The Ultimate Indian Cookbook

Meera Budhwar

CHARTWELL BOOKS, INC.

A QUANTUM BOOK

This edition published in 2011 by
CHARTWELL BOOKS, INC.
A division of BOOK SALES, INC.
276 Fifth Avenue, Suite 206
New York, New York 10001
USA

ISBN-13: 978-0-7858-2850-1

QUMTUIND

This book is produced by
Quantum Publishing
6 Blundell Street
London N7 9BH

Digitized by Quadrum Solutions, Mumbai, Indian
www.quadrumltd.com

Cover design by Dave Jones, www.euro-designs.info

Consultant Editors: Meera Budhwar and Caroline Smith
Managing Editor: Julie Brooke
Project Editor: Samantha Warrington
Assistant Editor: Jo Morley
Production Manager: Rohana Yusof
Publisher: Sarah Bloxham

Printed in Singapore by
Star Standard Industries Pte Ltd

The material in this publication previously appeared in *Complete Indian Cookbook,*
Indian Regional Cooking, Step-by-Step Indian Cooking and *Indian Vegetarian Cooking.*

Contents

Introduction

India is a land of spectacular contrasts, from the emerald Vale of Kashmir in the snow-clad mountains of the north to the steaming jungles and palm-fringed beaches of the tropical south. Across this vast country of more than a billion inhabitants the intricate use of spices unites all the kitchens of the land in producing food that is uniquely Indian.

There are about 25 spices on the shelf in the Indian pantry. Many of them will have come from the back garden along with fresh herbs and bulbs – onions, garlic and shallots. With this huge treasury of flavors the Indian cook can create an infinite number of different dishes. Spices can be used individually or combined, roasted or ground with water into a paste to produce flavors anywhere on the spectrum from sweet to sour, fiery to bland and fragrant to pungent.

Indians are almost intuitively aware of the medicinal properties of the herbs and spices they use to flavor their food, and they eat not just for sheer enjoyment and to stay alive, but to keep their bodies healthy and well tuned. Apart from their medicinal properties, spices and other condiments can be used to offset the extremes of temperature. In the north, warming spices take the bite out of freezing winter days, and in the south bittersweet tamarind has a soothing effect in the airless midday heat.

Of course what is eaten also depends largely on local produce. Broadly speaking, bread is eaten in the north and rice in the south. In the south the food tends to be more fiery (and paradoxically more refreshing, even if it does bring tears to the eyes). In Kerala, in particular, grow the coconut palms, the tamarind and jackfruit trees and the spice gardens that made Cochin rich and famous.

In the south, the tropical heat is put to use to mature pickles and for overnight fermentation of bread and cakes made from ground peas without the addition of yeast. Southerners often steam their food, whereas in the north it is oven cooked. In Rajasthan in the northwest, picnickers make an impromptu oven by digging a pit for a cow-dung fire on which they will cook spiced meat in a clay pot. The lid of the pot is sealed with dough, and more burning dung is heaped over it. This technique is called *dum* – food is baked slowly all the way through and all the juices are kept in, resulting in the tenderest meat and the richest possible flavor.

In Kashmir the winters are made bearable by cooking with warming spices, particularly cinnamon. People carry around baskets of live charcoal to keep the cold at bay between meals, and these baskets serve a dual purpose, often baking an egg or a potato for a hot snack.

Kashmir is a land of lakes and tranquil water gardens. The lakes produce abundant fish and delicious lotus roots. Ingenious farmers make floating vegetable gardens from reeds and mud, which can be towed about or left to drift picturesquely at anchor. When they are harvested, vegetables are sold from boats at the floating market. As autumn draws in there is a frenzy of mushroom picking and all kinds of vegetables, especially chilies, are hung up on the rafters to dry to keep the family supplied when the snows come. To see them through the winter, the Kashmiris make a dried spice cake called *ver*, crushing their spices according to a family recipe, then mixing them to a paste with mustard oil. The cake is hung up and bits are broken off it as required.

In the east, the Bengalis are noted for their love of fish and their insatiable desire for sweets, especially jaggery (raw sugar). Sugar cane is pressed to extract the juice, which is then heated over wood fires and patiently stirred for many hours until it is thick enough to set. Lumps of it are eaten as sweets and the Bengalis are so fond of it that they even manage to slip it into their vegetable curries.

Bombay in Maharashtra on the west coast, India's Hollywood and boom town founded on seven islands, has its own sweet treats – savory scones made of rice flour. They take several days and many processes to make, and are served at religious festivals.

Lucknow in Uttar Pradesh glories in whole chickens stuffed with quails, and a celebration halva made from the yolks of 100 eggs. Another local extravagance is a pearl pilaf – a dish of rice and "pearls" made by stuffing a chicken's esophagus with a mixture of egg yolks and real gold and silver, and tying it at intervals to resemble a string of pearls. It is then boiled and slit open, and the "pearls" pop out, looking very much like the real thing.

All over India, the laws of religion dictate what is eaten. Hindus are vegetarian, although the priestly caste of Kashmiri Brahmins do eat meat, abstaining instead from cooking with garlic and onions, which they believe inflame the passions. Jains are such strict vegetarians that they will neither eat root vegetables, for fear of killing insects as they dig, nor will they touch tomatoes or eggplants, whose color reminds them of blood. The Muslims will not eat pork and nowhere except in the state of Kerala is it permitted to kill a sacred cow. One sect of Muslims, the Bohris, alternate salty and sweet dishes and begin their meal by eating a pinch of salt in praise of Allah.

Presenting the meal

The traditional way to serve Indian food is on a *thali* or large tray, often of beautiful wrought metal. Each different dish is served in a small metal or earthenware bowl perched around the edge of the tray, or laid out on a low communal brass table. The diners sit on the floor, or on very low stools. The carpet is spread with

Below left: From the exuberance of the Palace of the Four Winds at Jaipur to the simplicity of the local post office, India is a subcontinent with many architectural delights.

Below right: For most of the time the elephant is a humble beast of burden, earning its keep by carrying and pulling heavy loads, but on festive occasions it is profusely decorated and becomes the center of much attention.

colored cloth to protect it and the guests are given giant colored napkins. The dishes can be wrapped in cotton or silk, which is loosely folded back over the food after it has been served. Often banana leaves will serve as disposable plates. More people today are sitting at a table with chairs, although in many parts the men are still served first, and then the women eat together on the floor in the kitchen.

Indians eat with their hands. Only the right hand is used – the left is thought to be unclean. In some parts of India the whole hand is used; in others just the fingertips. Generally, food is scooped up with a piece of flat bread in the north and mopped up with rice in the south. It means that cleanliness is very important – hands are washed before and after eating and water for washing is provided even on barrows selling snacks in the streets.

In all parts of India hospitality is legendary. All the dishes, including fruit and sweetmeats, are offered at once. Decoration is simple (nuts, chopped herbs, lemon slices) and sometimes exotic – silver- and gold-leaf *vark* on special occasions provides a direct, although expensive, source of minerals.

Cold water is drunk with meals. Breakfast, which might be a sweet flaky bread in the foothills of the Himalayas, a potato curry in the capital, Delhi, or a steamed bean cake (*idli*) in the south, is served with tea, sometimes spiced with cinnamon, or with hot strong coffee. During the day an Indian might drink freshly pressed fruit juice (mango is the favorite), coconut milk (in the south), or lassi, a sweet or sometimes salty drink made from yogurt. Muslims are forbidden alcohol, but there is plenty of potent liquor about for whose who want it. Other drinks include *asha*, which is distilled from jaggery, palm toddy and, of course, gin.

After a meal the hostess may offer betel leaves – glossy green leaves with mildly anesthetic properties and a refreshing taste. These are chewed and then spat out (or more delicately removed), like gum. They can be taken neat or wrapped around nuts, quicklime, cardamom pods, cloves or tobacco. Shah Jahan, one of Indian's more colorful rulers and the builder of the Taj Mahal as a mausoleum for his wife Mumtaz, was even known to wrap them around poison for his less-welcome guests.

This book offers enticing meat dishes from the north; from the east, characteristic fish delicacies. The vegetable dishes originate mainly in the south and west. From the south, too, come coconut, hot spicy vegetable dishes and legumes. This is a comprehensive collection of recipes: the flavor is wholly Indian.

Spices and aromatics in the Indian kitchen

Spices and aromatics are the very heart of Indian cooking. Flowers, leaves, roots, bark, seeds and bulbs (the simplest of natural ingredients) are used in endless combinations to produce an infinite variety of flavors: sweet, sharp, hot, sour, spicy, aromatic, tart, mild, fragrant or pungent.

The Indian cook aims to create blends of spices so subtle that a completely new taste arises – something indefinable. Sometimes the flavor of one particular spice can be magnified by the careful underplay of several others. As many as 15 spices may be used in one dish, or there might be only one. Spices, unlike herbs, can be used together without losing flavor.

It is best to buy your spices whole and grind them at home (see page 20) if the recipe calls for it. Whole spices keep longer than spice powders, which quickly lose their aroma. But even whole spices begin to taste tired after a while so buy small quantities and keep them in airtight jars in a cool, dark place. Do not buy curry powder – this is a blanket term for a blend of inferior spices, which will make everything taste the same.

Asafetida (Hing)

This is a resin that comes from Kashmir. It is bought ground and is said to smell of truffles. The flavor is quite pungent, but it is used mainly for its digestive properties, especially in the cooking of beans, where it combats flatulence. A pinch of it can be fried in hot oil before the rest of the ingredients are cooked.

Biriyani masala

This is a special sweet spice mix for biriyani dishes. Grind together the cardamom seeds from 8 pods, 25 g (1 oz) cinnamon stick, 6 cloves and 1 tsp fennel seeds.

Cardamom (Elaichi)

Pale green cardamom pods contain tiny black seeds and grow in the rainforests of southern India. They have a sweet fragrant flavor and can be used whole (although the pod is not usually eaten) or the seeds can be taken out of the pods and used separately. This takes time, but seeds are not usually sold out of their pods as they lose their flavor too quickly. Some recipes use ground cardamom seeds and as they are so small, it is best to grind them with a pestle and mortar.

Cayenne pepper (Pisi hui lal mirch)

Cayenne pepper, like paprika, comes from the seeds of plants in the capsicum family. It is a blend of various types of chili powder. The capsicum family is large, ranging from the sweet pepper to the chili. In general, the smaller the fruit, the hotter it is. Cayenne is sold as a powder. It should not be as hot as chili powder, but it is pretty hot and should therefore be used with care.

Chili (Mirchi)

Chili is the hottest flavor on earth. Chilies and chili powder should be used with extreme care. Do not take a bite of a chili or even lick one to see how it tastes as the effect will be quite devastating. Also, do not touch your mouth or eyes while handling chilies – the burning will be intense. Whole chilies can be seeded to make them a little less hot. Regulate the quantity of chili recommended in the recipes according to how much you can bear, and do not forget to tell your guests if you have left a whole chili lurking in the curry.

You can now buy fresh chilies at many grocery stores and supermarkets. If you live a long way from a regular supplier of chilies, buy them when you see them, wash them, dry them, put them in a jar and fill it to the brim with oil. Screw the lid on tightly and keep them in a cool, dark place. This is a very good way of storing them, and you get a flavored oil out of it too. Otherwise chilies go moldy quite quickly. If one is moldy, all the others will be infected too and all of them should be thrown away.

Chilies go red as they ripen, so dried chilies are always red. They are dropped into hot oil to release their aroma before other ingredients are added.

Chili powder is very hot indeed, as it is made from the crushed seeds of the chili, its hottest part. A blend of chili, garlic, cumin and oregano is sometimes also sold as chili powder.

Cinnamon (Dalchini)
Cinnamon has a rich, warm flavor. It is available as a powder but is much better bought in sticks. You can then break off a piece and add it to the curry. It should be discarded before serving. A lot of cinnamon is grown in Sri Lanka and it is the inner bark of a tree related to the laurel. The outer bark is scraped off and the inner bark peeled off in strips and rolled into sticks, which are then dried.

Cloves (Luong)
Cloves are the flower buds of an evergreen of the myrtle family. They have been used in India for thousands of years, not only in cooking, but also to sweeten the breath and relieve the pain of toothache. They contain a mild anesthetic. Cloves are best bought whole and ground, if necessary, at home with a pestle and mortar. Whole cloves are not eaten, but left on the side of the plate.

Coconut (Narial)
Fresh coconut may be grated and frozen. You can buy dried coconut in packets in Indian shops or supermarkets, and this can be used if the fresh variety is not available. (For how to prepare coconut, see page 18).

Cilantro (Dhaniya)
The English name for this spice comes for the Greek *koros*, meaning "bug." They are small ridged seeds, light brown in color, and can be easily squashed under the thumb. They are used powdered or whole.

Fresh green cilantro (Hari)
The leaves of the cilantro (cilantro) plant are rather like those of flat-leaf parsley, but darker and more brilliant. Fresh cilantro can be quite expensive to buy, but it is just as easily grown as parsley and can be used in the same way, in American as well as Indian dishes. The leaves have a very distinctive bittersweet taste. The best way of keeping this herb is in a jug of water in the fridge. Tired leaves can be revived by immersing in cold water for an hour, but do not keep them in water as they will go slimy.

Cumin (Jeera)
Cumin seeds are long and slim, similar to caraway seeds, but have a distinctive warm aroma. They are used either whole or ground, and can be bought ground. However, it is best to buy them whole and grind your own at home, as the ground spice loses its flavor quite quickly. Cumin is often used roasted. Drop the whole seeds into a hot dry saucepan and cook until the roasted fragrance emerges. Shake the saucepan to prevent sticking. The seeds can be stored whole, or ground in a coffee grinder and stored or used immediately.

Curry leaves (Kari pulia or Neem)
These are small greenish-grey leaves, a bit like bay, and are grown in many Indian gardens. They can be used fresh or dried; the dried ones can be crumbled onto food, and their aroma is released by its heat and moisture. They are sometimes fried in the oil the food is cooked in, and then discarded. They can also be eaten.

Food colorings
Turmeric and saffron will color food yellow, but you can also buy a vegetable coloring that has no taste. Red food coloring is used for tandoori chicken.

Fennel (Soonf)
Small oval seeds, greenish and with an aniseed flavor, these have digestive properties, and are sometimes served roasted at the end of an Indian meal. Used sparingly, they give warmth and sweetness to curries.

Fenugreek (Methi)
These tawny-colored seeds are chunky and very hard. Their bitter taste and aroma is released only by

cooking. In powdered form, fenugreek is one of the main ingredients of curry powder. It is used sparingly on its own. The leaves of the plant, which is related to spinach, are used in India as a herb.

Garam masala

Garam masala, meaning "hot spices," is a mixture of ground spices that is used sparingly, sprinkled either on a finished dish or onto the food just before it has finished cooking. It is far better to grind your own spices than to buy the ground mixture. Bought garam masala often contains inferior-quality spices and will not keep its flavor for long.

For homemade garam masala, grind together the cardamom seeds from 10 pods, 25 g (1 oz) cinnamon stick, 6 cloves and 6–8 whole black peppercorns. Store in an airtight jar in a cool place. (For preparing garam masala, see page 17).

Ghee

This is clarified butter and can be made at home (see page 16). The advantage of using ghee is that it can be heated to a very high temperature without burning, and so is useful for browning onions in order to give a sauce a good rich color, and for sizzling spices before the main ingredients are added to the pan. As the milk solids have been removed from ghee, it will keep well without being refrigerated. Many people prefer to use unsaturated fats and oils instead of ghee or butter.

Ginger

You can buy ginger ground (soondth) or fresh (adrak). The ground type is the same as that used in baking. The fresh "root" ginger is actually a rhizome, and is fawn in color and knobbly. Inside, the ginger is hard, yellow and fibrous. It is easiest to cook with once it is peeled and grated. You can also chop it if you are going to purée it with other ingredients. Fresh ginger can be kept wrapped in foil in the freezer or in a pot of sandy soil, kept fairly dry. It has quite a hot pungent flavor and should be used sparingly.

Mango powder (Amchur)

Unripe mangoes are sliced and dried, then powdered and sold as amchur. Amchur has a tart taste. If you are unable to find it, use a dash of lemon or lime instead.

Mustard seeds (Rai)

There are both white and black mustard seeds – the black contain a higher proportion of the volatile mustard oil. When dropped into hot oil, the mustard seeds pop, releasing their flavor. It is best to put a lid over the saucepan while you do this, or they will fly all over the kitchen. You can use this technique when pan-frying Western food to add extra aroma.

Nutmeg and mace (Jaiphal and Javitri)

Mace is the fleshy lattice-like covering of the nutmeg, which is golden brown in color. It is sold whole or powdered. Nutmegs are best bought whole and freshly grated at home.

Oil

Mustard oil, derived from the seeds of the mustard plant, is very popular with south Indian cooks, especially for pickling. This, and coconut oil, can be bought at specialist Indian groceries. Coconut oil is stirred together with a little warm water to release its aroma before use.

Peanut oil, also called arachide oil, is suitable for Indian cooking, as is the oil labeled simply "vegetable oil."

Paprika

Paprika is the ground seeds from a sweet red pepper. It is milder than chili powder or cayenne.

Peppercorns (Mirchi)

Peppercorns grow on large bushes in Malabar, on the west coast of India. They are picked by hand just before they are ripe, when they are still green, then left in the sun to dry and become black and crinkly. White peppercorns are the mature fruit, left to ripen on the bush, with the outer husk removed. This is traditionally done by immersing sacks of peppercorns in running streams. Bacteria get to work and loosen the husks, and the water finishes the job. The peppercorns are then stamped on in vats, like grapes, to rid them of the final traces of husk.

Black pepper is more aromatic; white pepper is stronger and hotter. Black pepper should always be bought whole and freshly ground over your food as it loses its aroma quickly.

Poppy seeds (Khus-khus)

It is the milky juice in the poppy's seed pod from which opium is derived – the seeds themselves have no narcotic properties. They are small, black and hard. There is also a white type.

Saffron (Zaffran)

Saffron is the most expensive spice of all. It is the filaments from a specially cultivated crocus – 75,000 stamens are needed to make 100 g (4 oz) of the spice. It is grown in Kashmir and used on festive occasions to give food a bright yellow color and a distinctive aroma. The filaments can be lightly roasted, crumbled in a little hot water and left to infuse to bring out their full strength. Buy saffron only from a reputable spice dealer or you may get an adulterated product, or something that is not saffron at all, especially if you buy it powdered.

Sambar powder

This is a delicious aromatic spice mix used in a number of recipes in this book.

100 g (4 oz) cilantro seeds
1 tsp asafetida
4 whole red chilies
6 curry leaves
25 g (1 oz) polished split black lentils (urid dal)
25 g (1 oz) channa dal
25 g (1 oz) fenugreek seeds
1 tbsp mustard seeds
4–6 whole black peppercorns

Roast the first four ingredients together and set them aside. Then roast each of the remaining ingredients separately. (Some take very little roasting before the fragrance emerges and would burn if roasted with the rest). Now grind all the roasted spices together in to a fine powder and store in a screw-top jar.

Tamarind (Amli)

A tamarind looks a little like a cinnamon-colored pod of broad beans. It grows on tall trees and is peeled and seeded when ripe. The fruit is then squashed into bricks and this is how you buy it. It has a very tart citric flavor and if you cannot find it, use a dash of lemon or lime instead. (For preparing tamarind juice, see page 16).

Turmeric (Haldi)

Turmeric is a rhizome related to ginger. Bought as a powder, it gives curries their characteristic golden yellow color. It has a delicate taste and is mildly antiseptic, although it becomes bitter if too much is used. Indians often use turmeric with beans because of its digestive properties.

Vindaloo paste

This is a very hot spicy paste. Chilies may be used with their seeds if you like particularly fiery food. In western India the Christians eat pork vindaloo. For those not permitted pork, vindaloo goes well with beef, lamb or prawns.

10 red chilies
50 g (2 oz) fresh ginger, finely grated
12 cloves garlic, 4 chopped and 8 thinly sliced
½ tsp fenugreek seeds
1 tsp mustard seeds
1 tsp cumin seeds
2–3 tbsp white wine vinegar
5–6 tbsp oil
225 g (8 oz) onion, chopped
450 g (1 lb) tomatoes
peeled cardamom seeds from 8 pods

Grind or pound the chilies, half of the ginger, chopped garlic, fenugreek, mustard and cumin, and mix them in to a paste with the vinegar. Do not add any water. Heat the oil and fry the onion until golden, then add the tomatoes and squash them into a paste as you cook. Stir in the spicy vinegar paste you have already made, add the remaining spices and fry until the oil runs out of them. The paste is then ready. Allow it to cool and store in an airtight container in a cool, dark place.

Legumes

There are many varieties of legume available in India and most of them can be found in the United States at Indian grocery stores and health food shops. Ahar dal, also called toor or toovar dal, is the main dal used in south India.

Moong dal *(Small, yellow, split legumes)* Beansprouts are made by sprouting these beans.

Masoor dal *(Split red legumes)* Salmon-colored, small, flat, round legumes which cook easily.

Channa dal These are similar to split peas, but slightly smaller.

Rajma *(Red kidney beans)* Large, dark red kidney-shaped beans. Should be soaked overnight to reduce cooking time.

Split black lentils *(Black gram)* The split urid dal is pale cream in color. It is usually soaked and ground to a paste. The bean is reddish-black in color, is very small in size and takes a long time to cook.

Lobia *(Black-eyed peas)* White, kidney-shaped beans with a black "eye." Popular in the north.

Mater *(Split peas)* Round, yellow legumes which are uniform in size.

Chole *(Chickpeas)* Beige, round, dried peas. Should be soaked overnight to reduce the cooking time. Chickpea flour is called gram, and is widely used in cooking.

Green moong dal *(Green lentils)* One of the more commonly used lentils. It can be used whole, split or polished to make various dals.

Special techniques

Adding spices to hot oil *(Baghar phoron)*
Oil is heated until it is very hot, and whole spices, crushed garlic or green chilies are added until the spices swell up or splutter or change color. This is then added to a cooked dish, or vegetables, or other spices are added and the cooking continues.

Dry roasting Place whole spices in a small, heavy-based frying pan and heat gently, stirring the spices constantly so that they do not burn. Soon the spices will turn a few shades darker and a lovely aroma will emerge.

Frying onions Place the oil in a frying pan or saucepan over medium high heat. When hot, add the onions, and, stirring occasionally, fry until the onions start to change color. Lower the heat and continue to fry until they are reddish brown.

Adding yogurt while cooking When a recipe calls for yogurt, always whisk the yogurt until smooth and add slowly, otherwise it curdles.

Peeling tomatoes Place the tomatoes in boiling water for 30 seconds. Drain and cool under running cold water. Peel, chop and use as required.

Cleaning chilies Pull out or slice off the stalks of the chilies and, holding them under cold running water, slit them open with a sharp knife and remove the seeds. The seeds are the hottest part of the chilies and most Indians do not remove them. Be very careful, when handling chilies, not to put your hands near your eyes as the oil will make them burn.

Chilies can be stored for 12–14 days by removing the stalk of each chili and putting them in a closed bottle in the fridge. When needed, wash the chilies and use as required.

SHELLING PISTACHIO NUTS

1 Pour boiling water over the nuts and leave for 30 seconds.

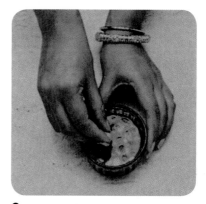

2 Drain and immerse in cold water.

3 The skin now peels away quite easily.

CLEANING A CHILI

1 Slice off the stalk end of the chili and hold it under cold running water. With a sharp knife, slit it open from top to bottom.

2 Remove all the seeds, keeping the chili under the running water to prevent the oil splashing into your eyes.

MAKING COCONUT MILK

1 Add hot water to the grated coconut.

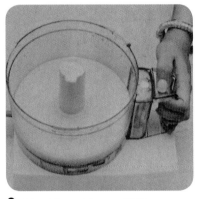

2 Blend the mixture until it is very smooth.

3 Pour through a sieve and collect the milk.

4 Squeeze the remaining milk out by hand.

Basic Recipes

Homemade Cottage Cheese
(Paneer)

3.5 l (7½ pt) milk
about 250 ml (8 fl oz) warm water
about 5 tbsp white vinegar

When adding the water and vinegar mixture to the milk, do not add more than necessary as this tends to harden the paneer. Use in savory or sweet dishes.

MAKING PANEER

1 Bring the milk to a boil and slowly add the water and vinegar.

2 Stop adding vinegar as soon as the milk curdles.

3 Strain the curdled milk through several layers of cloth.

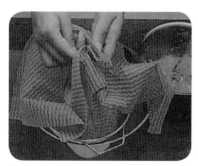

4 Tie the ends of the cloth and squeeze the liquid out.

5 Hang the cheese up to drain.

Yogurt
(Dahi)

Yogurt is used a great deal in Indian cooking to marinate meats and to give flavor to certain types of curry.

As yogurt is very refreshing and cool, it is eaten at most meals in certain parts of the country, particularly in the north. It is eaten either plain or with some seasoning or vegetables added to it. In Bengal, sweetened yogurt is eaten as a dessert.

On a hot day it can be mixed with water to make a refreshing drink called lassi.

Most families in India make their own yogurt at home, though it is easily available in the shops.

> 1.2 l (2½ pt) milk
> 2½ tbsp yogurt

1   Bring the milk to a boil, stirring constantly.
2   Remove from the heat and let it cool so that it feels barely warm.
3   Place the yogurt in a large bowl and whisk until smooth. Slowly add the lukewarm milk and stir gently. Cover the bowl and leave in a warm place overnight. Chill and use as required.

Once you have made some yogurt you can keep a little aside for the next batch, if you are going to make it within a day or two.

Clarified Butter
(Ghee)

> 450 g (1 lb) unsalted butter

Ghee can be bought at any Indian grocery store, but homemade ghee has a special flavor.

1   Heat the butter in a saucepan over low heat. Let it simmer until all the white residue turns golden and settles at the bottom.
2   Remove from the heat, strain and cool.
3   Pour into an airtight bottle and store in a cool place.

Keeps for 1–2 months.

Tamarind Juice
(Imli Ki Rus)

> 75 g (3 oz) dried tamarind
> 250 ml (8 fl oz) hot water

1   Soak the tamarind in the water for about 30 minutes.
2   Squeeze the pulp well to draw out all the juice. Strain and use as required.

By altering the amount of water, you can change the consistency.

Onion Mix
(Masala Mix)

2 large onions
3 tomatoes
3.5 cm (1½ in) ginger
5 cloves garlic
3–4 green chilies
4 tsp white vinegar

1 Blend all the ingredients together until you have a smooth paste.
2 Pour into an airtight bottle and keep in the fridge until needed. It will keep for up to two weeks.

Mixed Spice
(Garam Masala)

3 tbsp cardamom seeds
3 x 2.5 cm (1 in) pieces of cinnamon stick
1½ tsp cumin seeds
½ tbsp black peppercorns
½ tsp cloves
¼ of a nutmeg

1 Grind all the spices together until they are finely ground.
2 Store in a spice bottle until required.

The ingredients may be added in different proportions to according taste.

17

Coconut Milk
(Narial Ki Dudh)

When buying a coconut, shake it to make sure it is full of water. The more liquid it has, the fresher it is. (This liquid is not coconut milk, it is coconut water, and can be served as a drink when chilled).

To open the coconut Take a screwdriver and punch two holes in the eyes of the coconut and drain off all the liquid. Place in a preheated oven at 190°C/375°F/ Gas Mark 5 for 15–20 minutes. While the coconut is still hot, hit it with a hammer to split it and the flesh should come away from the shell.

To grate Peel off the brown skin from the coconut flesh and grate either with a hand grater or in a food processor.

To make coconut milk Combine the grated coconut with 500 ml (18 fl oz) of very hot water and blend. Pass this liquid through a sieve and squeeze the pulp to draw out all the liquid. This is known as thick coconut milk. The pulp is normally thrown away, but a few recipes may call for thin coconut milk, in which case the process is repeated using about 500 ml (18 fl oz) of hot water added to the coconut pulp. Blend the mixture and strain. Thick milk has a lot more flavor than thin milk.

A quick method of making coconut milk is to blend together 75 g (3 oz) of creamed coconut with 500 ml (17 fl oz) of hot water. Creamed coconut is available in supermarkets in 200 g (7 oz) portions. It keeps in the fridge for 2–3 months.

Roast Cumin
(Sukha Bhuna Jeera)

> 2 tbsp whole cumin seeds

1 Place the cumin seeds in a small saucepan over medium heat and dry roast them, stirring constantly. The seeds will turn a few shades darker. (Be careful not to burn them).
2 Cool and grind finely. Store in a spice bottle until required.

Cilantro seeds and dried red chilies can be roasted and ground in a similar manner and stored.

The Indian kitchen

Indian food can be cooked easily in a modern kitchen and you do not need to go out and buy a lot of equipment. However, you may be interested in some of the more traditional implements and utensils of the Indian kitchen.

Chula This is a hollow cube with a hole towards the bottom through which fuel is fed, and a hole at the top that acts as the gas burner. Midway there are four or five iron rods, which act as a bracket to hold the coal. The chula must have mud placed regularly on the inside and outside, so that it does not lose its shape. The mud is then left to dry out. There is a special technique to placing the mud, to ensure that after it dries out there are no cracks. In the cities, gas or electric cookers are often used instead.

Degchi This is a saucepan without handles, made of polished brass, stainless steel or other metals. The lid of the degchi is slightly dipped so that sometimes live coal can be placed on it to cook food slowly or keep food warm. Ordinary saucepans with lids can be used in the same way and the oven can be used to cook food slowly or to keep it warm.

Karai This is found in every Indian kitchen. It is a deep, concave metallic dish with two handles – one on each side. It looks like a Chinese wok but it is a little more rounded. It is used for deep frying. A deep fryer or saucepan or frying pan can be used if you do not have a karai.

Tava This is made from cast iron, is slightly concave, and is about 25 cm (10 in) in diameter. It is ideal for making chappatis or parathas as it distributes the heat evenly. A heavy-based frying pan will serve the same purpose.

Tongs These are used to remove a karai from the fire, or to remove a hot lid from a degchi. To remove the degchi from the fire it is normally held at either side with a cloth.

Metallic stirrers These are used in India as the pans are not non-stick. Use wooden spoons with non-stick pans. Wooden spoons are easier to use as they do not get hot, although if they are left in hot oil they tend to burn.

Below: Modern kitchen equipment, such as a food processor, garlic press and stainless steel knives, can be used to prepare many Indian dishes.

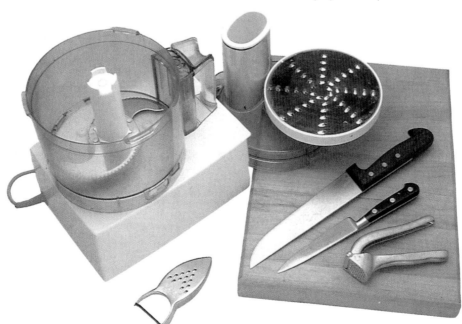

Thick stone slab This is used with a round stone roller like a rolling pin for grinding. Whole spices are ground with a little water; if dry ground spice is required a mortar and pestle is used. Legumes are also ground on the slab.

Tandoor This is a clay oven used in northern India. Tandoori chicken, whole or in pieces, and different kinds of breads and kebabs are baked in this oven. It is about 91 cm–1.2 m (3–4 ft) deep and about 60 cm (2 ft) wide on top, with a hole of 30 cm (12 in) diameter through which the food is put for cooking. It is fuelled by wood and coal and intensive heat builds up inside. This oven has mud patted on the inside and outside and it must be allowed to dry out. The chicken or the kebabs are marinated and then skewered and placed in the tandoor; the intensity of the heat cooks a whole chicken in a matter of minutes.

When bread is baked in a tandoor, the dough is slapped into the oven and when bubbles form, which is in a matter of a few seconds, the bread is cooked. It does not need to be turned over.

Tandoori chicken can be cooked easily in the modern oven, and then broiled for a few minutes to dry out. It is also excellent on the grill.

Electric coffee grinder In the modern kitchen, this can be used to grind spices. A blender or food processor may be used to blend onions, legumes and rice. The food processor can be used to make the dough for most of the breads and to save time when grating vegetables.

Below: Traditional kitchen equipment includes the karai, shown on the left of the picture with tongs to lift it from the heat and a wooden stirrer. The heavy frying pan and saucepan on the right are suitable modern substitutes for the tava and the degchi.

LEGUMES

India has over 60 types of legume, which provide a primary source of protein for her millions of vegetarians. When cooked, they can be left whole or puréed, making them extremely versatile as ingredients for curries, stuffings and patties. They can even be roasted or deep-fried for garnishes or snacks. To cook legumes, first pick them over and remove any foreign bodies. The larger varieties should be soaked overnight (at least 10 hours). If you are in a hurry, you can boil them for a couple of minutes and then take the saucepan off the heat and leave it to stand for an hour before cooking.

Split Peas with Vegetables I
(Kootu)

Serves 4
225 g (8 oz) yellow split peas, washed
900 ml (2 pt) water
½ tsp turmeric
1 tsp salt
75 g (3 oz) carrots, peeled and diced
50 g (2 oz) peas (fresh or frozen)
100 g (4 oz) green beans, cut into
    2.5 cm (1 in) lengths
I tbsp oil
1 tbsp urid dal
I tsp peppercorns
2 dried red chilies, broken in half
10–12 curry leaves
4 tbsp grated coconut
1 75 ml (6 fl oz) milk

Urid dal (*Black gram*) The bean is reddish-black in color and very small in size, and takes a long time to cook. The split urid dal is pale cream in color. It is usually soaked and ground into a paste.

1   Place the split peas, water, turmeric and salt in a saucepan and bring to a boil. Cover and simmer for about 35–40 minutes until the dal is soft. Add the vegetables and continue to cook until they are tender.
2   While the split peas are cooking, heat the oil in a small saucepan and fry the urid dal, peppercorns, red chilies, curry leaves and coconut until the dal and coconut turn golden. Grind into a paste.
3   When the dal and vegetables are cooked, add the paste and milk and continue to cook for 5–10 minutes. Serve hot with rice.

Split Peas Flavored with Garlic
(Rasam)

Serves 2
100 g (4 oz) yellow split peas
900 ml (2 pt) water
pinch of ground turmeric
1 tsp salt
2¼ tsp cumin seeds
1 tsp cilantro seeds
½ tsp peppercorns
3–4 diced red chilies
250 ml (8½ fl oz) tamarind juice (see page 16)
15 curry leaves
5 cloves garlic, crushed
1 tomato, chopped
1 tsp ghee (see page 16)

1   Wash the split peas in several changes of water and bring to a boil in a large saucepan with the measured amount of water, turmeric and salt. Cover, leaving the lid slightly open, and simmer for about 30 minutes until the dal is soft. Blend untll smooth.
2   In the meantime, dry roast 2 tsp cumin, cilantro, peppercorns and red chilies and grind finely.
3   Mix the tamarind juice, powdered spices, 10 curry leaves and garlic and bring to a boil. Simmer until it has reduced by half.
4   Add the cooked dal and tomato and simmer for 5 minutes.
5   In a small saucepan, heat the ghee until very hot, add the ¼ tsp of cumin seeds and the remaining curry leaves and let them sizzle for 5–6 seconds. Add to the cooked dal. Serve very hot with rice or as a soup.

Special Curried Chickpeas
(Channa Curry)

Serves 4

225 g (8 oz) chickpeas
1.2 l (2½ pt) water
½ tsp bakind soda
100 g (4 oz) butter or ghee
1 onion
2 or 3 bay leaves
cardamom seeds from 1 pod
2.5 cm (1 in) cinnamon stick
3 cloves
15 g (½ oz) fresh ginger, finely grated
1 tsp fennel seeds
3 cloves garlic, chopped
175 g (6 oz) tomatoes, peeled and chopped
1 tsp chili powder
1½ tsp ground cumin
leaves from 1–2 sprigs cilantro
½ tsp paprika
2 tsp ground coriander
1 tbsp lemon juice
salt

1. Pick over the chickpeas and wash thoroughly. Soak in water for at least 10 hours. Drain and cook in the measured water with the baking soda for 1½ hours, depending on the age of the peas, until tender but not soft.

2. Heat three-quarters of the butter or ghee in a good-sized saucepan and add the onion, bay leaves, cardamom seeds, cinnamon, cloves, ginger, fennel seeds, garlic and tomatoes. Fry until the onion is golden, squashing the tomato under the back of a wooden spoon to make a thick paste.

3. Add the chili powder, half the cumin, the cilantro leaves and paprika and cook for 3–4 minutes, stirring occasionally.

4. Add the cooked chickpeas with about 120 ml (4 fl oz) of their cooking liquor and cook over a low heat for 8–10 minutes.

5. In a separate pan, heat the remaining butter or ghee and when hot, add the remaining ground cumin. Fry for a few seconds, until the fragrance emerges, and add to the chickpeas.

6. Sprinkle on the ground coriander and lemon juice, and add salt to taste.

Steamed Rice and Lentil Cakes
(Idli)

Serves 4

90 g (3 oz) black lentils, washed
200 g (7 oz) rice, washed
good pinch of baking powder
pinch of salt

1 Soak the dal and rice separately in plenty of water for 4–5 hours. Drain.
2 In a bledner or food processor, grind the dal into a fine paste, adding a little water if necessary.
3 Grind the rice coarsely, adding a little water if necessary.
4 Mix the dal and rice together thoroughly, cover and then leave in a warm place overnight to let them ferment.
5 Mix in the baking powder and salt.
6 Fill the idli vessel* with the fermented mixture and steam for about 10 minutes until an inserted skewer comes out clean.

☼ *If you do not have an idli vessel, you can use egg poachers.*

Split Peas with Vegetables II (Sambar)

Serves 4

225 g (8 oz) yellow split peas, washed
1 l (2 pt) water
2 tsp salt
½ tsp ground turmeric
1½ tbsp oil
4 tsp cilantro seeds
1 tsp channa dal
1 tsp urid dal
6 dried red chilies
pinch of fenugreek seeds
good pinch of asafetida
350 g (12 oz) eggplant, cut into 1 cm (½ in) pieces
90 g (3 oz) green beans, cut into 4 cm (1½ in) lengths
6–8 shallots, peeled
120 ml (4 fl oz) tamarind juice (see page 16)
1 tsp mustard seeds
8–10 curry leaves

1 Place the toovar dal, water, 1 tsp of salt and turmeric in a large saucepan and bring to a boil. Lower the heat, cover, leaving the lid slightly ajar, and simmer for 35–40 minutes until the dal is soft.
2 In the meantime, heat ½ tbsp of oil in a small saucepan and fry the cilantro seeds, channa dal and urid dal, 4 dried red chilies, fenugreek and asafetida, stirring constantly, until golden. (Take care that they do not burn). Grind into a fine powder.
3 When the dal is soft, add the vegetables, tamarind juice and the remaining salt and continue to simmer until the vegetables are nearly tender.
4 Add the ground spices, stir well and cook for 5 minutes. Remove from the heat and put aside.
5 Heat the remaining 1 tbsp of oil in a small saucepan until very hot, add the mustard seeds and, when they stop spluttering, add the remaining dried red chilies, broken in half, and the curry leaves and let them fry for 4–5 seconds. Add this to the hot dal, stir well, and serve.

Stuffed, Spiced Pastries
(Kachori)

Serves 4
Filling
100 g (4 oz) black lentils, washed
1 tsp ghee (see page 16)
1 tsp salt
¼ tsp fennel seeds
1 cm (½ in) cinnamon stick
½ black cardamom pod, skinned
6 peppercorns
pinch of asafetida
pinch of ground ginger
¼ tsp ground cumin
½ tsp chili powder

Dough
225 g (8 oz) whole wheat flour
1 tsp salt
2 tsp ghee (see page 16)
120 ml (4 fl oz) hot water
oil for deep frying

1 To make the filling, soak the dal in plenty of cold water overnight.
2 Drain and blend into a smooth paste, adding a little water if necessary.
3 Heat the ghee in a karai, add the dal paste and salt and, stirring constantly, fry until the mixture leaves the side and forms a lump. Keep on one side.
4 Grind together the fennel, cinnamon, black cardamom and peppercorns into a fine powder.
5 Add this mixture and all the remaining spices to the dal and mix.
6 To make the dough, mix the whole wheat flour and salt.
7 Rub the ghee into the flour/salt mixture.
8 Add enough hot water to make a soft, pliable dough. Knead for about 10 minutes.
9 Divide the dough into 12–14 balls.
10 Take one ball, flatten slightly and make a depression in the middle with your thumb, to form a cup shape. Fill the center with the spiced dal mixture and re-form the pastry ball, making sure that the edges are well gathered. Flatten the ball slightly between the palms of your hands.
11 Heat the oil in a karai over medium heat and fry the kachoris a few at a time for 7–8 minutes until they are lightly browned. Serve with pickles.

Fried Lentil Cake Curry
(Dhokkar Dalna)

Serves 4

150 g (5 oz) channa
   dal, soaked
   overnight in
   900 ml (2 pt) water
   and drained
¾ tsp salt
½ tsp ground turmeric
1 cm (½ in)
   ginger, grated
2 tbsp dried coconut
2 green chilies
150 ml (5 fl oz) water
200 ml (7 fl oz) oil
3 medium potatoes,
   cut into 2.5 cm

(1 in) pieces
½ tsp whole
   cumin seeds
2 bay leaves
1 tsp ground turmeric
½ tsp chili powder
1½ tsp ground cumin
1 tsp ground coriander
½ tsp salt
2 tomatoes, chopped
350 ml (12 fl oz) water
1 tsp ghee (see page
   16)
½ tsp garam masala
   (see page 17)

1 Mix the drained dal with the salt, turmeric, ginger, coconut, green chilies and 5 fl oz water in a blender until you have a smooth creamy mixture.

2 In a karai, heat 120 ml (4 fl oz) of the oil over medium heat and fry the dal mixture until it leaves the sides and forms a ball. Spread 1 cm (½ in) thick on a greased plate. Cool. Cut into 2.5 cm (1 in) squares.

3 Heat the rest of the oil in a karai over medium heat and fry the dal squares a few at a time until golden brown. Set aside.

4 Fry the potatoes until lightly browned. Set aside.

5 Lower the heat to medium, add the whole cumin seeds and bay leaves and let them sizzle for a few seconds.

6 Add the turmeric, chili powder, cumin, cilantro, salt and tomatoes and fry for 2 minutes. Add the water and bring to a boil.

7 Add the potatoes, cover and cook for 10 minutes. Add the fried dal squares, cover again and cook until the potatoes are tender.

8 Add the ghee and sprinkle on garam masala. Remove from the heat. Serve hot with rice or pilaf.

Lentils cooked with Fish Heads
(Mooror Dal)

Serves 4
225 g (8 oz) green lentils
about 1.5 l (3 pt) water
¼ tsp ground turmeric
1 tsp salt
4 tbsp oil
2 fish heads, quartered
3 green chilies,
2 dried red chilies
1 medium onion, chopped
¼ tsp chili powder
4 cardamom pods
5 cm (2 in) cinnamon stick
2 bay leaves
good pinch of sugar

1 Dry roast the lentils, stirring constantly, until golden brown.
2 Wash the lentils in several changes of water. Bring them to a boil in the measured amount of water with the turmeric and salt.
3 Throw away the foam, lower the heat, cover, leaving the lid slightly open, and simmer for about 1 hour. Put aside.
4 Heat the oil in a saucepan and fry the fish heads until golden brown.
5 Drain the fish heads and add to the lentils. Put the remaining oil aside. Bring the lentils to a boil again, add the green chilies, lower the heat and simmer for about 15 minutes.
6 In a small pan, heat the remaining oil again until very hot. Add the dried red chilies and fry for 4–5 seconds. Add the onion and stirfry until golden brown.
7 Add the chili powder, cardamom, cinnamon, bay leaves and sugar and fry for a few seconds.
8 Add to the lentils and stir thoroughly.

Curried Chickpeas with Coconut
(Channa Curry)

Serves 4
225 g (8 oz) chickpeas
4–5 tbsp butter or ghee (see page 16)
1 tsp mustard seeds
1 onion, finely chopped
1 tbsp finely grated fresh ginger
1 green chili, chopped
4–6 curry leaves
75 g (3 oz) grated fresh coconut
salt

1 Pick over the chickpeas, wash thoroughly and soak in water for at least 10 hours. Cook in fresh water for 1–1½ hours, depending on the age of the chickpeas, until tender but not soft.
2 Heat the butter or ghee in a saucepan and add the mustard seeds. Let them sizzle for a few seconds until they have all popped.
3 Add the onion and fry until golden.
4 Drain the chickpeas, reserving the cooking liquid. Add the chickpeas to the saucepan with the ginger, green chili and about 2 tbsp cooking liquor. Cover and cook over low heat, stirring occasionally, for 10 minutes, until the chickpeas have absorbed the flavors of the sauce.
5 Stir in the curry leaves and grated coconut and add salt to taste.

Dal Curry I

Serves 2
175 g (6 oz) toovar dal
900 ml (2 pt) water
2 tbsp oil
½ tsp mustard seeds
½ tsp cumin seeds
1 small onion, finely chopped
leaves from 1–2 sprigs cilantro
2 tomatoes, peeled and chopped
½ tsp turmeric
1 clove garlic, finely chopped
2 green chilies, sliced
salt

1 Pick over the dal and wash it well. Bring the water to a boil, add the dal and simmer for about 15 minutes, until you can crush the dal with the back of a wooden spoon. Set aside, covered.

2 Heat the oil in a frying pan and add the mustard seeds. Sizzle for a few seconds until all the seeds have popped.

3 Add the cumin seeds, onion and half the cilantro leaves and fry, stirring, until the onion is golden.

4 Add the tomato, turmeric, garlic and chili, stirring well and mashing the tomato with the spices to make a paste.

5 Add the dal with a little of its cooking water. Stir well, heat through and add salt to taste. Garnish with the remaining cilantro leaves.

Dal and Mushroom Curry (Kumban Dal)

Serves 4
225 g (8 oz) red lentils (masoor dal)
1.2 l (2½ pt) water
1½ tsp turmeric
175–225 g (6–8 oz) button mushrooms, halved
15 g (½ oz) fresh ginger, finely grated
1 green chili, sliced
225 g (8 oz) onion, chopped
1 tbsp sambar powder (see page 11)
2 tbsp grated or dried coconut
225 g (8 oz) tomatoes, peeled and chopped
2 tbsp oil
1 tsp mustard seeds
4–6 curry leaves
salt

1 Pick over the dal and wash it thoroughly. Cook in the water with the turmeric for 10–15 minutes, until it can be crushed under the back of a wooden spoon.

2 Add the mushrooms, ginger, chili and half of the onion, and cook for a further 10 minutes.

3 Meanwhile, blend the sambar powder with the coconut in a blender, add to the curry with the tomato and cook for a further 6–8 minutes, until the sauce is thick and smooth.

4 Heat the oil in a pan, add the mustard seeds and let them sizzle for a few seconds until they have all popped.

5 Add the curry leaves and remaining onion and fry until the onion is golden. Add to the curry with salt to taste.

Dal Curry II

Serves 4

350 g (12 oz) toovar dal
1.2 1 (2½ pt) boiling water
50 g (2 oz) butter or ghee (see page 16)
1 green pepper, sliced
½ tsp cumin seeds
1–2 green chilies, chopped
1½ tbsp gram (chickpea) flour
salt
leaves from 1 sprig of cilantro, finely chopped

1. Pick over the dal and wash it well. Add to the water and simmer for 10–15 minutes until soft. Strain off excess water and mash well or blend in a blender. Set aside.
2. Heat the butter or ghee in a pan and when hot, fry the green pepper until soft. Add the cumin seeds and green chili for a few seconds until their flavor emerges. Add to the dal.
3. In a small bowl, mix the gram flour with 2–3 tbsp water until it forms a smooth paste.
4. Stir the paste into the dal and simmer on low heat, stirring occasionally, for about 5 minutes, until it is thick and soupy.
5. Stir in salt to taste and garnish with cilantro.

Red Lentils with Fried Onions
(Masoor Dal)

Serves 2

200 g (7 oz) red lentils, washed
1 l (2 pt) water
¼ tsp ground turmeric
1½ tsp ground cumin
2 tomatoes, chopped
½ tsp salt
2–3 green chilies
1 tbsp cilantro leaves, chopped
3 tbsp ghee (see page 16)
3 cloves garlic, crushed
1 onion, finely sliced

1 Bring the lentils to a boil in the measured amount of water in a large saucepan. Remove any foam that forms.
2 Add the turmeric, cumin and tomatoes, and mix with the lentils.
3 Lower the heat, partially cover and simmer for about 40 minutes until tender. Add the salt, chilies and cilantro leaves and mix in with the lentils. Remove from the heat.
4 In a small pan, heat the ghee. Add the garlic and onion and fry until golden brown.
5 Pour over the lentils and serve with rice.

Dal and Coconut Curry
(Dal Narial)

Serves 2

175 g (6 oz) toovar dal
900 ml (2 pt) water
1½ tsp turmeric
½ tsp chili powder
1 small onion, finely chopped
2–3 tbsp grated coconut
1 tomato, peeled and chopped
2 tbsp oil
1 tsp mustard seeds
4–6 curry leaves
salt

1 Pick over the dal and wash it well. Bring the water to a boil, add the dal and simmer for 10–15 minutes, until soft and mushy.
2 Stir in the turmeric and chili powder, cover and keep hot over a low heat.
3 Put half the onion with the coconut in a blender, add 1 tbsp water and blend until smooth. Stir into the dal with the tomato.
4 Heat the oil in a saucepan and add the mustard seeds. When all the seeds have popped, add the remaining onion and fry until golden. Add to the dal.
5 Stir in the curry leaves and salt to taste.

Green Lentil Curry I
(Moong Dal)

Serves 2

200 g (7 oz) whole green lentils (moong dal)
1.4 l (3 pt) water
¼ tsp ground turmeric
1 tsp ground cumin
2 tomatoes, chopped
1 tsp salt
1 tbsp ghee (see page 16)
¾ tsp whole cumin seeds
2 dried red chilies
2 bay leaves
2.5 cm (1 in) cinnamon stick
4 green cardamom pods

1 Heat a saucepan and dry roast the lentils, stirring constantly until all the lentils turn light brown.
2 Wash the lentils in several changes of water and bring to a boil in the measured amount of water in a large saucepan. Skim off any foam that forms.
3 Lower the heat, add the turmeric, cumin, tomatoes and salt and partially cover and simmer for about 1 hour 15 minutes until the lentils are soft.
4 In a small pan, heat the ghee over medium heat, add the cumin seeds, red chilies, bay leaves, cinnamon stick and cardamom pods and let them sizzle for a few seconds.
5 Add the hot ghee and spices to the lentils and stir. Serve with rice.

Spicy Lentils
(Aamti)

Serves 4

200 g (7 oz) toovar dal, washed
900 ml (2 pt) water
pinch of turmeric
1 tsp salt
1 tbsp oil
½ tsp mustard seeds
1 clove garlic, crushed
½ tsp whole cumin seeds
120 ml (4 fl oz) tamarind juice
2 tbsp cilantro leaves, chopped

1 Place the toovar dal, water, turmeric and salt in a large saucepan and bring to a boil.
2 Cover, leaving the lid slightly open, and simmer the dal for about 40–45 minutes until tender. In a food processor or blender, blend the dal until smooth; return to the saucepan.
3 Heat the oil in a small saucepan. Add the mustard seeds, garlic and cumin seeds and fry until the mustard seeds start to splutter.
4 Add the tamarind juice and bring to a boil, stirring constantly. Add to the dal and mix. Boil for 5 minutes.
5 Garnish with the cilantro leaves and serve hot.

Lentils with Spicy Dumplings
(Dal Dhokri)

Serves 4

2 green chilies	pinch of turmeric
1 cm (½ in) ginger	pinch of asafetida
225 g (8 oz) toovar dal, washed	½ tsp salt
900 ml (2 pt) water	1 tbsp oil
½ tsp ground turmeric	about 4 tbsp hot water
1 tsp salt	½ tsp mustard seeds
½ tsp sugar	½ tsp whole cumin seeds
2–3 tbsp lime juice	good pinch of cinnamon
Dough	2 tbsp grated coconut
225 g (8 oz) whole wheat flour	2 tbsp chopped cilantro leaves
1 tbsp gram flour	1 tbsp ghee (see page 16)
½ tsp chili powder	

1 Grind the chilies and ginger together into a paste.
2 Place the toovar dal, water, turmeric, salt and chili and ginger paste in a large saucepan and bring to a boil. Cover and simmer for 40–45 minutes until the dal is tender. Add the sugar and lime juice and mix. Remove from the heat and put aside.
3 Sieve the whole wheat flour, gram flour, chili powder, turmeric, asafetida and salt. Rub in the oil.
4 Add enough water to make a stiff dough. Knead for 8–10 minutes until soft and smooth.
5 Divide into 4 portions. Flatten each portion slightly and roll into a round 20 cm (8 in) across. Cut into small diamond shapes.
6 In a small saucepan, heat the oil, add the mustard and cumin seeds and, as soon as the seeds start to splutter, add cinnamon and fry for 2–3 seconds. Add to the dal.
7 Add the small dough pieces to the dal, bring to a boil for 12–15 minutes, stirring occasionally. (Add a little water if the dal gets too thick).
8 Garnish with the coconut, cilantro and ghee.

Green Lentil Curry II
(Moong Curry)

Serves 2

175 g (6 oz) whole green lentils (moong dal)
100 g (4 oz) butter or ghee
1 onion, finely chopped
1 green chili, chopped
2 cloves garlic, chopped
15 g (½ oz) fresh ginger, finely grated
100 g (4 oz) tomatoes, peeled and chopped
½ tsp turmeric
½ tsp chili powder
leaves from 1 sprig of cilantro
1 tsp cumin seeds
salt

1 Pick over the lentils, wash thoroughly and soak in water for about 4 hours. Drain and cook in fresh water to cover for about 30 minutes, until tender.
2 Meanwhile, heat three-quarters of the butter or ghee in a pan, add the onion, green chili, garlic and ginger and fry until the onion is golden.
3 Add the tomato and cook, mashing it under the back of a wooden spoon to make a paste.
4 Add the turmeric, chili powder and cilantro leaves and continue to cook until the fat runs clear of the spices.
5 Add the lentils and about 2 tbsp of their cooking liquid and cook for a further 5 minutes.
6 Meanwhile, fry the cumin seeds in the remaining butter or ghee for a few seconds, until the fragrance emerges, then add to the lentils. Add salt to taste.

Dry Sprouted Green Lentil Toran
(Moong Dal Toran)

Serves 4

2 tbsp oil
¼ tsp asafetida
1 tsp chili powder
½ tsp turmeric
1 tsp ground coriander
½ tsp ground cumin
450 g (1 lb) sprouted green lentils
salt
leaves from 1 sprig of cilantro
1 tsp lemon juice

1 Heat the oil in a pan, add the asafetida, chili powder, turmeric, ground coriander and cumin, and fry for a few minutes until the fragrance emerges.
2 Add the sprouted lentils together with 2 tbsp water, ½ tsp salt and half the cilantro leaves. Cook, covered, on low heat, stirring occasionally, for about 10 minutes or until the sprouted lentils are cooked and almost all the water has evaporated.
3 Sprinkle on the lemon juice and the remaining cilantro leaves. Add extra salt to taste.

Bengal Gram Dal
(Channa Dal)

Serves 2

200 g (7 oz) channa dal, washed

1.4 l (3 pt) water

1½ tbsp ghee (see page 16)

¾ tsp whole cumin seeds

2 bay leaves

2 dried red chilies

5 cm (2 in) cinnamon stick

4 cardamom pods

¾ tsp ground turmeric

½ tsp chili powder

1¼ tsp ground cumin

1 tsp salt

½ tsp sugar

2 tbsp dried coconut

1 tbsp raisins

1 Bring the dal and water to a boil in a large saucepan over medium heat. Skim off any foam that forms.

2 Lower the heat, partially cover the saucepan and simmer for about 1 hour 15 minutes until soft.

3 Heat the ghee in a small saucepan over medium heat, add the whole cumin seeds, bay leaves, red chilies, cinnamon stick and cardamom pods and allow them to sizzle for a few seconds.

4 Add the turmeric, chili powder, ground cumin, salt and sugar and stirfry for 1 minute. Add the dried coconut and raisins and fry for another 1–2 minutes.

5 Mix the ghee and spices with the dal and stir. Serve with rice or deep fried white bread (see page 108) and spicy potatoes (see page 61).

Green Lentil and Plantain Curry
(Kela Moong Curry)

Serves 2

175 g (6 oz) whole green lentils (moong dal)

900 ml (2 pt) water

1 or 2 plantains, peeled and sliced

½ tsp turmeric

1 green chili, chopped

salt

100 g (4 oz) grated or dried coconut

½ tsp ground cumin

2 tbsp oil

1 tsp mustard seeds

4–6 curry leaves

1 Pick over the lentils, wash thoroughly and cook in the water for about 30 minutes until nearly done.

2 Add the plantain, turmeric, chili and ½ tsp salt, and continue to cook over low heat.

3 In a blender, blend the coconut with the cumin and 1–2 tbsp water to make a thick paste. Add to the lentils. Stir and cook for 3 minutes to heat through. Add a little water, if necessary, to make a thick sauce.

4 Heat the oil in a frying pan and when hot, add the mustard seeds and the curry leaves. Let them sizzle for a few seconds until all the seeds have popped, then add to the curry. Add extra salt to taste.

Split Peas with Vegetables
(Dal Tarkari)

Serves 4

200 g (7 oz) split peas, washed
750 ml (1½ pt) water
2 tbsp ghee (see page 16)
½ tsp whole cumin seeds
2 bay leaves
2–3 green chilies, cut lengthways
275 g (10 oz) potatoes, cut into
   2.5 cm (1 in) pieces
75 g (3 oz) peas
350 g (12 oz) cauliflower, cut into large florets
½ tsp ground turmeric
1 tsp salt

1 In a large saucepan, bring the split peas and water to a boil. Cover and simmer for 30 minutes. Remove from the heat.

2 Heat the ghee in a large saucepan over medium heat. Add the cumin seeds, bay leaves and green chilies and let them sizzle for a few seconds.

3 Add the potatoes, peas and cauliflower and fry for 1–2 minutes.

4 Add the boiled split peas with the water, turmeric and salt. Mix thoroughly, lower the heat and cook until the vegetables are tender. (If the dal gets too thick, add a little more water).

Black-eyed Peas with Onions
(Lobia Aur Pyaz)

Serves 2

200 g (7 oz) black-eyed peas, washed
1.2 l (2½ pt) water
2 tbsp oil
1 large onion, finely chopped
2 cloves garlic, crushed
5 mm (¼ in) ginger, grated
1–2 green chilies, finely chopped
½ tsp salt
1 tsp corn syrup

1 Soak the peas in the water overnight.
2 Boil the peas in the water and then cover and simmer for 1 hour until tender. Drain.
3 Heat the oil in a large saucepan and fry the onion, garlic, ginger and chili until the onions are soft.
4 Add the peas, salt and corn syrup and cook until all the moisture is absorbed, about 15 minutes. Serve with chappatis (see page 106).

Spiced Chickpeas
(Masala Channa)

Serves 4

225 g (8 oz) chickpeas
100 g (4 oz) butter or ghee (see page 16)
1 onion, finely chopped
2 cloves garlic, finely chopped
1 tbsp finely grated fresh ginger
225 g (8 oz) peeled and chopped tomatoes
½ tsp ground coriander
½ tsp chili powder
1 tbsp mango powder (amchur)
½ tsp ground cumin
1 tsp garam masala (see page 17)
leaves from 1 sprig of cilantro
salt

1 Pick over the chickpeas, wash thoroughly and soak in water for at least 10 hours. Drain and cook in fresh water for 1–1½ hours, depending on the age of the chickpeas, until tender but not soft.
2 Heat the butter or ghee in a pan, add the onion, garlic and ginger and fry until the onion is golden.
3 Add the tomato, cilantro, chili powder, mango powder, cumin, garam masala and half of the cilantro leaves. Cook, stirring briskly to mash the tomato with the back of the spoon into a paste.
4 Drain the chickpeas, reserving the cooking liquid, and add to the saucepan with 2 tbsp of the liquid. Cover and cook over low heat, stirring occasionally, for about 10 minutes, until the chickpeas have absorbed the flavors of the spices.
5 Sprinkle on the remaining cilantro leaves and add salt to taste.

Soured Chickpeas
(Chole)

Serves 4

200 g (7 oz) chickpeas, washed
900 ml (2 pt) water
1 teabag
3 tbsp oil
225 g (8 oz) potatoes, boiled and diced
   into 1 cm (½ in) cubes
2 medium onions, finely chopped
1 clove garlic, crushed
1 cm (½ in) ginger, grated
2 tsp ground coriander
2 green chilies, chopped
1½ tbsp mango powder (amchur)
½ tsp chili powder
¾ tsp salt
175 ml (6 fl oz) water
1½ tsp garam masala (see page 17)

1 Soak the chickpeas in the water with the teabag overnight.
2 Discard the teabag and place the chickpeas and the water in a saucepan and bring to a boil. Cover and simmer for about 1 hour until tender. Drain.
3 Heat the oil in a saucepan over medium heat and fry the diced potatoes until lightly browned. Set aside.
4 In the remaining oil, fry the onions until golden brown. Add the garlic and ginger and fry for 2 minutes.
5 Add the chickpeas, cilantro, green chilies, mango powder, chili powder, salt and potatoes and stirfry for about 2 minutes until well mixed.
6 Add the water and cook for about 15 minutes. Sprinkle with garam masala. Serve hot with Yogurt Bread (see page 110).

Curried Red Kidney Beans
(Masala Rajma)

Serves 4
200 g (7 oz) red kidney beans, washed
1.2 l (2½ pt) water
6 tbsp oil
2 bay leaves
5 cm (2 in) cinnamon stick
3 green cardamom pods
1 large onion, finely sliced
2 cloves garlic, crushed
1 cm (½ in) ginger, grated
¾ tsp ground turmeric
½ tsp chili powder
½ tsp salt
2 tomatoes, chopped
120 ml (4 fl oz) water

1 Soak the beans in the water overnight.
2 Boil the beans in the water and then cover and simmer for 1 hour until tender. Drain.
3 Heat the oil in a large saucepan over medium heat and add the bay leaves, cinnamon and cardamom pods and let them sizzle for a few seconds. Add the onion, garlic and ginger and fry until the onions are golden brown.
4 Add the turmeric, chili powder, salt and tomatoes and fry for 1 minute. Add the drained beans and fry with the spices for 2–3 minutes.
5 Add 120 ml (4 fl oz) water and bring to a boil, stirring occasionally. Cover, lower the heat and cook for 10–15 minutes. Serve with Chappatis (see page 106).

Whole Black Beans
(Mahan Ki Dal)

Serves 2
175 g (6 oz) whole black beans (sabut urid)
1 cm (½ in) ginger, grated
3 dried red chilies
4 cloves garlic, crushed
1½ tsp salt
1.5–1.75 l (3 – 3½ pt) water
3 tbsp yogurt, lightly beaten
4 tbsp ghee (see page 16)
1 small onion, chopped
1 tbsp cilantro leaves, chopped

1 Wash the beans in several changes of water.
2 Place the beans, ginger, chilies, garlic, salt and water in a large saucepan and bring to a boil. Lower the heat, cover, leaving the lid slightly ajar, and simmer for about 3–3½ hours until the beans are soft. (Add more water if required).
3 Mash the beans slightly and add the yogurt and 1 tbsp of the ghee. Cook for a further 30 minutes. (When the beans are cooked they should turn reddish-brown in color and the consistency should be thick).
4 Heat the remaining ghee and fry the onion until lightly golden. Add this to the hot beans and garnish with the cilantro leaves.

VEGETABLES

India grows a huge variety of vegetables, and the combinations of vegetables and spices are endless. Sometimes the spices are used to make a thick sauce, and at other times the vegetables are cooked "dry" *(toran)* so that the spices stick to them, making a tasty, crunchy "crust." Hot spicy vegetables are usually served with rice and mild fragrant ones with bread.

Ripe Mango Curry
(Aam Curry)

Serves 4

4 small sweet ripe mangoes, cubed,
   with the skins left on
600 ml (1 pt) water
2 tsp chili powder
½ tsp turmeric
salt
grated flesh of ½ coconut
½ tsp ground cumin
6 curry leaves
2 tbsp oil
2 tsp mustard seeds
2 tsp fenugreek seeds
2 red chilies, cut into 4 pieces
2–3 tsp sugar

1 Cook the mango in the water with the chili powder, turmeric and 1 tsp salt for about 5 minutes, making sure that the mango does not lose its shape.

2 Blend the coconut with the cumin and add to the mango with half of the curry leaves.

3 Heat the oil in a frying pan and when hot, add the mustard seeds. Let them sizzle for a few seconds until they have all popped, then add the fenugreek seeds, red chili and remaining curry leaves. Stir and fry for a few seconds, then add to the mango. Stir well and add sugar and salt to taste.

Buttermilk Curry
(Kalan)

Serves 4–6

225 g (8 oz) sweet potato, peeled and cubed
1 green plantain, peeled and cubed
225 g (8 oz) white pumpkin, peeled and cubed
½ tsp turmeric
½ tsp chili powder
grated flesh of 1 small coconut
½ tsp ground cumin
½ tsp ground white pepper
600 ml (1 pt) buttermilk, made by stirring 3 tbsp water into 225 g (8 oz) yogurt
2 green chilies, cut in half
2 tbsp oil
1 tsp mustard seeds
2 red chilies, cut into 3 or 4 pieces
½ tsp fenugreek seeds
8 curry leaves
2 tbsp sugar
2 tsp salt

1 Cook the sweet potato, plantain and pumpkin in water to cover with the turmeric and chili powder, over low heat for about 10 minutes, until tender but not soft.
2 Blend the coconut, cumin and white pepper and mix well with the buttermilk, then add to the saucepan with the vegetables and green chilies. Heat through on low heat for 3–4 minutes, stirring briskly to prevent the buttermilk from separating.
3 Heat the oil in a pan, add the mustard seeds, red chili, fenugreek seeds and half of the curry leaves and let them sizzle for a few seconds, until all the seeds have popped.
4 Stir into the curry with the remaining curry leaves, and add sugar and salt to taste.

Stuffed Vegetables
(Sambharia)

Serves 4

2 long eggplants
6 small potatoes, peeled
6 small onions, peeled
5 green chilies
1 cm (½ in) ginger
175 g (6 oz) gram flour
1 tbsp ground coriander
½ tsp ground cumin
pinch of ground turmeric
1 tsp salt
¾ tsp sugar
about 120 ml (4 fl oz) oil
2 tbsp lime juice
¾ tsp mustard seeds
good pinch of asafetida
2 tbsp coconut, grated
2 tbsp cilantro leaves, chopped

1 Wash the vegetables and dry thoroughly.
2 Cut the eggplants into 4 cm (1½ in) slices.
3 Make 2 cuts crossways on each vegetable; cut about three-quarters of the way down the length, but do not cut all the way through.
4 Grind 2 green chilies and the ginger into a paste.
5 Make a paste by mixing the gram flour, cilantro, cumin, turmeric, salt, sugar, 2½ tbsp oil, lime juice and the chili and ginger paste.
6 Carefully open the slits in the vegetables and stuff them with this paste. If you have any paste left over after stuffing the vegetables, add it to the vegetables while they are frying.
7 In a large, heavy-based frying pan, heat the remaining oil, add 3 green chilies, broken in half, mustard seeds and asafetida and let them sizzle for 8–10 seconds.
8 Add the vegetables carefully, cover and fry over a low heat, occasionally stirring gently. When one side is done, turn the vegetables over, and cover and cook the other side. Add a little more oil if necessary. Serve hot, garnished with the coconut and cilantro.

Mixed Vegetables
(Choch Chori)

Serves 4

1 medium potato, peeled	1 tsp panch phoron
200 g (7 oz) white radish, scraped	2 bay leaves
1 small eggplant	¾ tsp ground turmeric
225 g (8 oz) pumpkin, peeled	½ tsp chili powder
275 g (10 oz) cauliflower stalks	½ tsp mustard seeds, ground
4 tbsp oil	½ tsp salt
2–3 dried red chilies, broken in half	½ tsp sugar
	120 ml (4 fl oz) water

1 Cut the potato into 8 pieces lengthways.
2 Quarter the white radish lengthways and cut into 4 cm (1½ in) pieces.
3 Cut off the stalk from the eggplant and quarter lengthways. Cut into 4 cm (1½ in) pieces.
4 Cut the pumpkin into 2.5 cm (1 in) cubes.
5 Cut the cauliflower stalks into very thin strips 6 cm (2½ in) long.
6 Heat the oil in a karai or saucepan over medium heat, add the dried chilies and fry until they become brownish black (about 4–5 seconds).
7 Add the panch phoron and bay leaves and let them sizzle for a few seconds.
8 Add all the vegetables and fry for 3–4 minutes, stirring constantly.
9 Add the turmeric, chili powder, mustard seeds, salt and sugar and mix thoroughly with the vegetables.
10 Lower the heat to medium, cover and cook for 10 minutes.
11 Remove the cover, give the vegetables a good stir and then add the water. Bring to a boil, cover again and cook for about 10–15 minutes, until all the vegetables are tender and all the water has evaporated.

Vegetable Curry with Roast Coconut
(Eliseri)

Serves 2–3

100 g (4 oz) toovar dal
1.2 l (2½ pt) water
450 g (1 lb) pumpkin, cubed
1 tsp chili powder
½ tsp turmeric
salt
50–75 g (2–3 oz) grated or dried coconut
1 tsp ground cumin
6–8 curry leaves
3 tbsp oil
1 tsp mustard seeds
2 red chilies, cut into pieces

1 Pick over the dal, wash it thoroughly and cook in the water for about 15 minutes, until you can mash it under the back of a wooden spoon.
2 Meanwhile, cook the pumpkin in water for about 12 minutes, until tender.
3 Drain the dal and the pumpkin, reserving a little of the cooking liquid, and mix the two together with the chili, turmeric and ½ tsp salt. Cook over low heat, stirring, for 3–4 minutes, adding a little of the cooking liquid if the mixture threatens to stick. Cover and set aside.
4 Blend half the coconut with the cumin and half the curry leaves. Stir into the curry.
5 Heat the oil in a frying pan and when hot, add the mustard seeds and red chili. Let them sizzle for a few seconds until all the mustard seeds have popped. Add the remaining grated coconut and curry leaves and fry, stirring briskly, for a few seconds until the fragrance of roast coconut emerges.
6 Fold the fried spice mixture into the curry and add salt to taste.

Vegetable Curry with Coconut Milk
(Sabzi Narial)

Serves 4
flesh of 1 coconut, grated
450 g (1 lb) ripe pumpkin, peeled and sliced
2 carrots, peeled and sliced
1 tbsp coconut oil, mixed with 1 tbsp water
4–6 curry leaves
salt

1 Blend the coconut in a blender with 1 tbsp boiling water. Transfer to a piece of muslin and squeeze out the milk into a bowl. Return the coconut to the blender, add another tbsp boiling water and repeat the process, straining the milk into a separate bowl.
2 Cook the sliced pumpkin and carrots in water to cover on low heat for about 10 minutes until tender, then add the second bowl of coconut milk and bring to a boil. Remove the saucepan from the heat.
3 Stir in the first bowl of coconut milk, add the coconut oil, curry leaves and salt to taste.

Vegetables in a Yogurt and Coconut Sauce
(Avial)

Serves 4
2 plantains, peeled and cut into 1 cm (½ in) pieces
100 g (4 oz) green beans, cut into 1 cm (½ in) pieces
50 g (2 oz) carrots, diced into 5 mm (¼ in) cubes
50 g (2 oz) peas
¾ tsp chili powder
½ tsp ground turmeric
¾ tsp salt
350 ml (12 fl oz) water
250 ml (8 fl oz) natural yogurt
2 green chilies, chopped
1 tsp ground coriander
2 tbsp dried coconut
1 tbsp oil
½ tsp whole mustard seeds
6–8 curry leaves

1 Place the plaintains and vegetables, chili powder, turmeric, salt and water in a large saucepan and bring to a boil. Simmer for about 20 minutes until the vegetables are tender. Remove from the heat.
2 Whisk the yogurt, green chilies, cilantro and coconut together and set aside.
3 In a large saucepan heat the oil over medium heat. Add the mustard seeds and curry leaves, and after 5–6 seconds add the vegetables with the liquid. Cook for 2–3 minutes. Lower the heat and add the yogurt mixture and, stirring occasionally, cook for a further 4–5 minutes. Serve with rice.

Vegetable Curry, Kerala Style
(Sambar)

Serves 4–6

350 g (12 oz) toovar dal

1.2 l (2½ pt) water

½ tsp turmeric

100–175 g (4–6 oz) okra, trimmed and
    cut into 2.5 cm (1 in) lengths

3 tbsp oil

1 medium onion, quartered and sliced

225 g (8 oz) potatoes, cubed

2 tomatoes, peeled and chopped

2 tbsp tamarind juice (see page 16)

75–100 g (3–4 oz) grated coconut

4–6 curry leaves

2 tbsp sambar powder (see page 11)

1 tsp mustard seeds

1 red chili, cut into 4 pieces

salt

cilantro leaves, to garnish

1. Pick over the dal, wash it thoroughly and cook in the water with the turmeric for about 15 minutes, until you can mash it under the back of a wooden spoon.

2. Meanwhile, fry the okra in 1 tbsp oil, turning gently, until all the oil is absorbed. This seals the okra and helps it keep its shape. Set aside.

3. When the dal is ready, stir in the onion and potato and continue to cook gently on low heat for about 8 minutes, until the vegetables are half cooked.

4. Add the tomato and okra and cook for a further 10 minutes, until the vegetables are tender, adding a little extra water if the pot threatens to boil dry.

5. Stir in the tamarind juice, cover and keep hot.

6. Fry the coconut and half of the curry leaves in 1 tbsp oil, then blend with the sambar powder and add to the vegetables.

7. Heat the remaining oil, add the mustard seeds and the red chili and let them sizzle for a few seconds until all the mustard seeds have popped. Add to the curry.

8. Stir in salt to taste and garnish with cilantro leaves.

Vegetable Curry, Tamil Style
(Sambar)

Serves 4–6

350 g (12 oz) toovar dal
1.2 l (2½ pt) water
1 eggplant
2 medium potatoes
1 medium onion, quartered and sliced
½ tsp turmeric
salt
3–4 tbsp tamarind juice (see page 16)
3 tbsp sambar powder (see page 11)
1 tomato, cut into 8 pieces
1 tbsp oil
1 tsp mustard seeds
4–6 curry leaves
2 tsp sugar
leaves from 1 sprig of cilantro

1 Pick over the dal, wash it thoroughly and cook in the water for about 15 minutes, until you can mash it under the back of a wooden spoon.
2 Meanwhile, peel the eggplant and potatoes and cut into cubes, dropping them in a saucepan of water as you go to prevent discoloration.
3 Add the eggplant, potato and onion to the cooked dal, with a little extra water if necessary, and cook for about 8 minutes, until the vegetables are half cooked.
4 Add the turmeric and ½ tsp salt, and continue cooking for about 10 minutes, until the vegetables are tender.
5 Stir in the tamarind juice, sambar powder and tomato, cover and keep hot.
6 Heat the oil in a saucepan and add the mustard seeds and curry leaves. Let them sizzle for a few seconds, until all the mustard seeds have popped, then add to the curry.
7 Stir in sugar and salt to taste and garnish with cilantro leaves.

Spicy Mustard Leaves
(Sarson Ki Saag)

Serves 4

450 g (1 lb) mustard leaves
225 g (8 oz) spinach
2–3 green chilies, chopped
1 tsp salt
120 ml (4 fl oz) water
about 2 tbsp cornstarch
2 tbsp ghee (see page 16)
1 onion, finely chopped
1 cm (½ in) ginger, grated
4 cloves garlic, crushed
4 tbsp butter

1 Wash the greens and chop finely.
2 Place the greens, chilies, salt and water in a large saucepan and cook on a low heat, stirring occasionally. A lot of water will be given off by the greens, but if all the moisture dries up before the greens are cooked, add a little more water. Cook until the greens are tender and all the moisture has evaporated.
3 Place this mixture in a food processor or blender and blend to a purée without adding any more water.
4 After blending, add enough cornstarch and mix the purée to the desired consistency.
5 Heat the ghee in a large frying pan, add the onion, ginger and garlic and fry until lightly golden.
6 Add the puréed greens and, stirring constantly, cook for about 3–4 minutes over medium heat.
7 Put in a serving dish with the butter on top. Serve with corn meal bread (see page 108).

Spinach Toran
(Palak Toran)

Serves 2

450 g (1 lb) fresh
spinach
4 tbsp oil
1 small onion, finely
chopped
1 green chili, chopped

75 g (3 oz) tomatoes,
peeled and
chopped
75 g (3 oz) grated or
dried coconut
salt

1 Wash the spinach, discard any discolored leaves and tough stalks, and shake dry. Chop as finely as possible and leave in a colander to drain.
2 Heat the oil in a saucepan and gently fry the onion and green chili until the onion is transparent.
3 Add the spinach and tomato, cover tightly and cook on low heat for 4–5 minutes, shaking the saucepan occasionally, until the spinach has wilted.
4 Stir in the coconut and add salt to taste.

Peas and Cauliflower with Ginger
(Mater Gobi)

Serves 2

3 tbsp oil
25 g (1 oz) ginger, cut
into very thin strips
1 small cauliflower,
broken into
large florets

225 g (8 oz) peas
1 tsp ground turmeric
1 tsp salt
2 tbsp cilantro leaves,
chopped

1 Heat the oil in a karai or saucepan over medium heat. Add the ginger and fry, stirring constantly, until slightly browned.
2 Add the cauliflower, peas, turmeric and salt and mix with the ginger.
3 Lower the heat, cover and, stirring occasionally, cook for about 20–25 minutes until the vegetables are tender.
4 Garnish with the cilantro leaves.

Spinach with Legumes and Vegetables
(Sai Bhaji)

Serves 2

50 g (2 oz) channa dal,
washed
600 ml (1 pt) water
3 tbsp oil
1 medium onion, finely
chopped
1 cm (½) in ginger,
grated
2 cloves garlic,
crushed

250 g (9 oz) spinach,
washed and
chopped
1 medium potato,
diced into 1 cm
(½ in) cubes
3 tomatoes, chopped
50 g (2 oz) peas
½ tsp ground turmeric
½ tsp chili powder
1 tsp ground coriander
½ tsp salt

1 Bring the dal to a boil in the water over high heat. Cover and simmer for about 40 minutes until the dal is tender. Drain and save the liquid; make it up to 350 ml (12 fl oz) with water, if necessary.
2 Heat the oil in a large saucepan over medium high heat and fry the onion, ginger and garlic until soft.
3 Add the cooked dal and the rest of the ingredients and stirfry for 2–3 minutes. Add the liquid, cover, lower the heat to medium low and cook for about 30 minutes.

Spinach with Paneer
(Saag Paneer)

Serves 2

4 tbsp oil

175 g (6 oz) paneer (see page 15), drained and cut into 1 cm (½ in) cubes

1 large onion, finely sliced

4 cloves garlic, crushed

1 cm (½ in) ginger, grated

350 g (12 oz) frozen spinach, chopped

½ tsp ground turmeric

¾ tsp chili powder

1 tsp ground coriander

¾ tsp salt

1 Heat the oil in a karai over medium high heat and fry the paneer until brown. Set aside.

2 Add the onion, garlic and ginger to the remaining oil and fry until golden.

3 Add the thawed spinach, turmeric, chili powder, cilantro and salt and fry for 2–3 minutes.

4 Lower the heat to medium, cover and cook for 10 more minutes.

5 Add the fried paneer and, stirring constantly, cook until dry.

Cabbage with Peas
(Bund Gobi Aur Mater)

Serves 4
3 tbsp oil
2 bay leaves
¾ tsp whole cumin seeds
700 g (1½ lb) cabbage, finely shredded
1 tsp ground turmeric
1 tsp chili powder
1½ tsp ground cumin
1 tsp ground coriander
2 tomatoes, chopped
¾ tsp salt
½ tsp sugar
100 g (4 oz) peas

1 Heat the oil in a karai over medium high heat and add the bay leaves and the cumin seeds. Let them sizzle for a few seconds.
2 Add the cabbage and stir for 2–3 minutes.
3 Add the turmeric, chili powder, cumin, cilantro, tomatoes, salt and sugar and mix with the cabbage.
4 Lower the heat, cover and cook for 15 minutes. Add the peas and cover again. Continue to cook for 15 more minutes, stirring occasionally.
5 Remove the cover, turn the heat up to medium high and, stirring continuously, cook until dry.

Paneer with Peas
(Mater Paneer)

Serves 4
6 tbsp oil
275 g (10 oz) paneer (see page 15), drained and cut into 1 cm (½ in) pieces
6 tbsp Onion Mix (see page 17)
1 tsp ground turmeric
½ tsp chili powder
1 tsp ground coriander
¾ tsp salt
175 g (6 oz) peas
250 ml (8 fl oz) water
1 tbsp cilantro leaves, chopped (optional)

1 Heat the oil in a karai over medium high heat and fry the paneer pieces until golden brown. Remove and drain on paper towels.
2 In the remaining oil add the onion mixture and fry for 3 minutes, stirring constantly. Add the turmeric, chili powder, cilantro and salt and continue to fry for 2–3 more minutes.
3 Add the peas and mix thoroughly. Add the water and bring to a boil. Cover, lower the heat to medium low and simmer for 5 minutes. Gently add the pieces of fried paneer and simmer a further 10 minutes. Garnish with the cilantro leaves and serve hot.

Dry Peas
(Sukka Mater)

Serves 4

2 tbsp oil

5 cm (2 in) ginger, cut into very thin strips

700 g (1½ lb) peas (fresh or frozen)

1 tsp salt

½ tsp mango powder (amchur)

1 Heat the oil in a karai or saucepan over a medium high heat and fry the ginger, stirring constantly, until slightly browned.

2 Add the peas and salt and mix with the ginger.

3 Lower the heat, cover and cook for about 15 minutes until the peas are tender.

4 Add the mango powder, mix and remove from the heat.

Cabbage with Coconut
(Bund Gobi Aur Narial)

Serves 4

2 tbsp oil

2 bay leaves

¾ tsp whole cumin seeds

1–2 green chilies, chopped

700 g (1½ lb) cabbage, shredded

¾ tsp salt

⅓ tsp sugar

3 tbsp dried coconut

½ tsp ground cumin

1 Heat the oil in a karai over medium high heat and add the bay leaves, cumin seeds and the green chilies and let them sizzle for a few seconds.

2 Add the cabbage, salt and sugar and mix. Cover, lower the heat to medium and cook for about 15 minutes until half-done.

3 Add the coconut and ground cumin and fry, stirring constantly for 10–15 minutes, until all the moisture has evaporated.

Dry Spiced Cabbage
(Gobi Bhaji)

Serves 4
450 g (1 lb) cabbage
225 g (8 oz) potatoes
2 tbsp oil
½ tsp ground cumin
½ tsp ground coriander
½ tsp turmeric
¼ tsp asafetida
½ tsp chili powder
salt

1 Cut the cabbage into strips, and peel and finely chop the potatoes.
2 Heat the oil and fry the cumin, cilantro, turmeric, asafetida and chili powder for 3–4 minutes, until the fragrance of the spices emerges.
3 Add the cabbage and potato, sprinkle on 1–2 tbsp water and ½ tsp salt, cover the saucepan tightly and cook on low heat for 5–6 minutes, until the potato is cooked.
4 Take the pot off the heat and let it stand, covered, for 3–4 minutes. Add extra salt to taste.

Cabbage Toran
(Gobi Toran)

Serves 2
2 tbsp oil
1–2 tsp polished split black lentils (urid dal)
½ tsp mustard seeds
4–6 curry leaves
1 small onion, finely chopped
1 green chili, sliced
15 g (½ oz) fresh ginger, finely shredded
450 g (1 lb) cabbage, very finely chopped or grated
½ tsp turmeric
50–75 g (2–3 oz) grated coconut
salt

1 Heat the oil in a large pan, big enough to hold the cabbage. Add the dal and fry until golden.
2 Add the mustard seeds and let them sizzle for a few seconds until they have all popped.
3 Add the curry leaves, onion, green chili and ginger and continue to fry, stirring, for 3–4 minutes.
4 Stir the cabbage into the saucepan with the turmeric, cover tightly and cook for about 4 minutes on low heat until tender but not soft.
5 Stir in the grated coconut and add salt to taste.

Carrot Toran
(Gajar Toran)

Serves 2
50 g (2 oz) toovar dal
225 g (8 oz) carrots, peeled and diced
salt
2 tbsp oil
1 tsp mustard seeds
4 curry leaves
1 or 2 green chilies, seeded and sliced
75 g (3 oz) grated or dried coconut

1 Pick over the dal, wash thoroughly and cook in water to cover for 15 minutes, until it can be crushed under the back of a wooden spoon and almost all the water has been absorbed.
2 Cook the carrots in salted water to cover for 10 minutes, until just tender. Drain and add to the dal.
3 Heat the oil in a saucepan and when hot, add the mustard seeds, curry leaves and chili. Let them sizzle for a few seconds until all the seeds have popped, then add to the carrots.
4 Stir in the coconut and heat through over low heat for 2–3 minutes, stirring, until the curry is quite dry. Add salt to taste.

Green Papaya Toran
(Papaya Toran)

Serves 2
450 g (1 lb) unripe green papaya,
   peeled and cubed
salt
2 tbsp oil
2 tsp polished split black lentils (urid dal)
1 small onion, finely chopped
1 tsp mustard seeds
4–6 curry leaves
1 red chili, cut into 4 or 6 pieces
100 g (4 oz) grated or dried coconut

1 Cook the papaya in salted water to cover for 10–15 minutes, until tender but not soft. Drain and keep hot.
2 Heat the oil in a frying pan and add the dal, onion, mustard seeds, curry leaves and red chili. Fry until the onion is golden, then add the papaya, then stirfry for 3–4 minutes.
3 Stir in the grated coconut and add salt to taste.

Green Bean Toran I
(Hari Moong Toran)

Serves 2

1 tbsp oil
1 tsp mustard seeds
1 red chili, cut into 4 or 6 pieces
4–6 curry leaves
1 small onion, finely chopped
225 g (8 oz) green beans, trimmed and cut into
  2.5 cm (1 in) lengths
salt
50–75 g (2–3 oz) grated coconut

1 Heat the oil in a heavy-based saucepan and when hot, add the mustard seeds. Let them sizzle for a few seconds until they have all popped.
2 Add the red chili, curry leaves and onion and fry gently, stirring, until the onion is golden.
3 Turn the heat to low and add the beans, 1 tbsp water, ½ tsp salt and the coconut. Cook, with the lid firmly on, for about 10 minutes, until the beans are tender but not soft, stirring occasionally.
4 Let the pot stand for about 5 minutes and add extra salt if necessary before serving.

Green Bean Toran II
(Hari Moong Toran)

Serves 2

1 or 2 green chilies, chopped
75 g (3 oz) grated coconut
4–6 curry leaves
1 clove garlic, chopped
225 g (8 oz) green beans, trimmed and
  cut into 2.5 cm (1 in) lengths
1 tsp turmeric
2 tbsp oil
2 tsp polished split black lentils (urid dal)
1 tsp mustard seeds
salt

1 Crush the green chili with the coconut, curry leaves and garlic and mix with the green beans and turmeric in a heavy-based saucepan. Add 1–2 tbsp water and cook over very low heat, covered tightly, for 10–15 minutes, until tender. Stir occasionally to prevent sticking.
2 Heat the oil in a pan, add the dal and fry until golden.
3 Add the mustard seeds and let them sizzle for a few seconds until they have all popped. Add to the beans and cook for 3–4 more minutes.
4 Let the pot stand off the heat, covered, for 3–4 minutes, then add salt to taste.

Beans with Coconut
(Sukhi Bean Aur Narial)

Serves 4
3 tbsp oil
½ tsp nigella seeds
2–3 dried red chilies
450 g (1 lb) green beans washed and cut into
   2.5 cm (1 in) lengths
2 tbsp dried coconut
½ tsp salt

1 Heat the oil in a karai over medium high heat,
   add the nigella seeds and chilies and let them
   sizzle for a few seconds.
2 Add the beans and stirfry for 10 minutes.
3 Add the coconut and salt and mix in thoroughly
   with the beans. Stirring constantly to avoid sticking,
   cook 5–7 more minutes. Serve with Poori (see
   page 112).

Vegetable Paneer
(Paneer Bhiyia)

Serves 2
2 tbsp oil
1 medium onion, finely chopped
1 clove garlic, crushed
275 g (10 oz) paneer (see page 15), drained
½ tsp ground turmeric
½ tsp salt
1 small green pepper, seeded and cut into
   1 cm (½ in) pieces
1 large tomato, chopped
1–2 green chilies, chopped
1 tbsp cilantro leaves, chopped

1 Heat the oil in a karai over medium heat and
   fry the onion and garlic for 5 minutes.
2 Add the paneer, turmeric and salt and stirfry for
   5 minutes.
3 Add the green pepper and tomato and cook for
   8–10 minutes, stirring occasionally.
4 Sprinkle with the green chilies and cilantro leaves
   and remove from the heat. Serve with Poori (see
   page 112).

Potatoes with Fenugreek Leaves
(Aloo Methi)

Serves 2
450 g (1 lb) potatoes
handful fresh fenugreek leaves or
   1 tbsp dried fenugreek leaves
3 tbsp ghee (see page 16)
½ tsp ground turmeric
1 tsp ground cumin
½ tsp chili powder
1 tsp salt

1 Wash the potatoes and then peel and cut them into 2 cm (¾ in) cubes.
2 If you are using fresh fenugreek, remove the tough lower stalk, wash the leaves thoroughly and chop finely. If you are using dried fenugreek, soak it in water for about 20–25 minutes, gently squeeze the water out and chop the leaves. Remove any tough stalks.
3 Heat the ghee in a large frying pan. Add the potatoes and, stirring constantly, fry for about 3–4 minutes.
4 Add the turmeric, cumin, chili powder and salt to the potatoes and cook for a further minute.
5 Add the fenugreek leaves and mix with the potatoes. Lower the heat, cover and, stirring occasionally, cook for about 20 minutes until the potatoes are tender. Add 1–2 tbsp of water if necessary.

Potato and Green Papaya Curry
(Aloo Peper Dalna)

Serves 4
6 tbsp oil
450 g (1 lb) green papaya, peeled, seeded
   and cut into 2.5 cm (1 in) cubes
450 g (1 lb) potatoes, peeled and cut into
   2.5 cm (1 in) cubes
1 tsp whole cumin seeds
2 bay leaves
2 tomatoes, chopped
¾ tsp ground turmeric
½ tsp chili powder
1½ tsp ground cumin
¾ tsp salt
large pinch of sugar
300 ml (10 fl oz) water
2 tsp ghee (see page 16)
½ tsp garam masala powder (see page 17)

1 Heat the oil in a karai or saucepan over medium high heat.
2 Fry the papaya, a few pieces at a time, until slightly brown. Remove and set aside.
3 Fry the potatoes, a few pieces at a time, until slightly brown. Remove and set aside.
4 Lower the heat to medium, add the cumin seeds and bay leaves and let them sizzle for 3–4 seconds. Add the tomatoes and fry for 1–2 minutes.
5 Add the turmeric, chili powder, cumin, salt and sugar and mix with the tomatoes and fry for one more minute.
6 Add the papaya and potatoes and mix well with the spices. Add the water and bring to a boil. Cover and cook for 15–20 minutes until the vegetables are tender.
7 Add the ghee and garam masala before removing from the heat.

Potato Masala Curry
(Aloo Masala)

Serves 4

3 or 4 medium potatoes, cubed
1 large onion, finely chopped
½ tsp turmeric
salt
2 green chilies, chopped
2 tsp garam masala (see page 17)
2 tbsp grated or dried coconut
15 g (½ oz) fresh ginger, finely grated
2 tbsp oil
1 tsp mustard seeds
4–6 curry leaves
leaves from 1 sprig of cilantro

1 Cook the potato in just enough water to cover with three-quarters of the onion, the turmeric, ½ tsp salt and the green chili, for about 8 minutes, until half cooked.

2 Meanwhile, blend the garam masala, coconut and ginger in a blender. Add to the potato and continue to cook for 8 more minutes, until tender but not soft.

3 Heat the oil in a frying pan and add the mustard seeds. Let them sizzle for a few seconds until they have all popped, then add the remaining chopped onion and fry until golden. Stir into the curry.

4 Add salt to taste and sprinkle on the curry and cilantro leaves.

Potatoes with Poppy Seeds
(Aloo Posto)

Serves 2

3 tbsp oil
450 g (1 lb) potatoes, diced into 2 cm (¾ in) pieces
2 tbsp poppy seeds, ground
1 tbsp dried coconut
¾ tsp salt
a big pinch of sugar
2–3 green chilies, chopped

1 Heat the oil in a karai over medium heat and fry the potatoes, stirring occasionally until nearly done, about 15 minutes.
2 Add the poppy seeds, coconut, salt, sugar and green chilies and continue cooking until the potatoes are tender. Serve with rice.

Ripe Plantain Curry with Yogurt
(Kela Dahi)

Serves 4

2 or 3 ripe plantains, peeled and thickly sliced
600 ml (1 pt) water
½ tsp chili powder
½ tsp turmeric
4–6 tbsp grated or dried coconut
½ tsp cumin seeds or ground cumin
225 g (8 oz) yogurt
2 tbsp oil
1 tsp mustard seeds
1 red chili, cut into 3 or 4 pieces
6–8 curry leaves
2–3 tbsp brown sugar
salt

1 Cook the plantain in the water with the chili powder and turmeric for 5 minutes, until tender but not soft, and most of the water has evaporated.
2 Grind or pound the coconut with the cumin (or blend in a blender), then mix with the yogurt.
3 Stir the yogurt into the plantain over low heat for 3–4 minutes, stirring all the time. Set aside.
4 Heat the oil in a saucepan and when hot, add the mustard seeds. Let them sizzle, then add the red chili and half of the curry leaves. Continue to fry for a few seconds, then add to the curry.
5 Stir in sugar and salt to taste and sprinkle with the remaining curry leaves.

Potatoes with Tamarind
(Imli Aloo)

Serves 4

6 tbsp oil
1 tsp whole cumin seeds
2 large onions, finely chopped
4 cloves garlic, crushed
700 g (1½ lb) small potatoes, peeled and boiled
1 cm (½ in) ginger, grated
½ tsp ground turmeric
¼ tsp chili powder
¾ tsp salt
1 tsp sugar
75 ml (3 fl oz) thick tamarind juice (see page 16)
½ tsp roast ground cumin (see page 18)

1 Heat the oil in a karai over medium high heat, add the cumin seeds and let them sizzle for a few seconds.
2 Add the onions and garlic and fry them until the onions are soft.
3 Lower the heat to medium low, add the potatoes and grated ginger and fry for 5–7 minutes, stirring occasionally.
4 Add the turmeric, chili powder, salt, sugar and tamarind juice and cook for 10–15 minutes.
5 Before removing from the heat, sprinkle with the roast ground cumin.

Potatoes with Green Peppers and Coconut
(Aloo Aur Capsicum)

Serves 2

3 tbsp oil

½ tsp whole mustard seeds

pinch of asafetida

6–8 curry leaves

450g (1 lb) potatoes, boiled, peeled and diced
into 1 cm (½ in) cubes

1 green pepper, seeded and cut into
1 cm (½ in) pieces

3 tbsp dried coconut

½ tsp salt

2 green chilies, chopped

1 tbsp cilantro leaves, chopped

1 Heat the oil in a karai over medium heat, add the mustard seeds, asafetida and curry leaves and let them sizzle for 3–4 seconds.

2 Add the potatoes and green pepper and stirfry for 5 minutes.

3 Add the coconut and salt and, stirring occasionally, cook for another 5–7 minutes.

4 Before removing from the heat, sprinkle with the chilies and cilantro leaves. Serve hot with Poori (see page 112).

Dry Potatoes
(Sukha Aloo)

Serves 2–3

700 g (1½ lb) potatoes, washed

4 tbsp oil

1 tsp cumin seeds

pinch of asafetida

¾ tsp ground turmeric

¾ tsp chili powder

1 tsp ground coriander

1 tsp mango powder (amchur)

1 tsp salt

1. Boil the potatoes with the skins still on. Peel and cut into large pieces (do not overcook them).
2. Heat the oil in a karai or saucepan over medium high heat. Add the cumin seeds and asafoetida and let them sizzle for about 5–6 seconds.
3. Add the turmeric, chili powder, cilantro, mango powder and salt and fry for 5–7 seconds. If it starts to stick, sprinkle a little water on the mixture.
4. Add the potatoes and, stirring gently, fry for 5 minutes.

Spicy Potatoes
(Rasadar Aloo)

Serves 2–3

700 g (1½ lb) small potatoes

2–3 medium tomatoes

4 tbsp oil

1 tsp cumin seeds

pinch of asafetida

¾ tsp ground turmeric

1 tsp ground coriander

¾ tsp chili powder

1 tsp paprika

1 tsp salt

300 ml (10 fl oz) water

½ tsp garam masala (see page 17)

2 tbsp cilantro leaves, chopped

1. Peel the potatoes and wash them.
2. Place the tomatoes in boiling water for 10 seconds. Carefully peel and chop them.
3. Heat the oil over medium high heat in a karai or saucepan. Add the cumin seeds and asafetida and let them sizzle for 5–6 seconds.
4. Add the chopped tomatoes, turmeric, cilantro, chili powder, paprika and salt and, stirring constantly, fry for 30 seconds. (If it starts to stick to the bottom, sprinkle on a little water).
5. Add the potatoes and fry for 2–3 minutes, stirring constantly.
6. Add the water and bring to a boil. Lower the heat, cover and cook for about 15 minutes until the potatoes are tender.
7. Add the garam masala and mix.
8. Remove and garnish with the cilantro leaves.

Cauliflower with Potato and Tomatoes
(Aloo Gobi Tamatar Masala)

Serves 4

75 g (3 oz) potato
450 g (1 lb) cauliflower
50 g (2 oz) butter or ghee (see page 16)
1 small onion, finely chopped
15 g (½ oz) fresh ginger, finely grated
1 clove garlic, finely chopped
2 green chilies, cut into 4–6 pieces
leaves from 1 sprig of cilantro
100 g (4 oz) tomatoes, peeled and chopped
½ tsp chili powder
½ tsp turmeric
½ tsp ground coriander
½ tsp fennel seeds
½ tsp garam masala (see page 17)
1 tsp ground cumin
salt

1   Peel the potato and cut into chunks. Divide the cauliflower into florets, discarding the tough stalks. Put the vegetables in a saucepan of cold water to prevent discoloration.

2   Heat three-quarters of the butter or ghee in a heavy-based saucepan and add the onion, ginger, garlic, green chili and half the cilantro leaves. Stir and fry until the onion is golden.

3   Stir in the tomato, add the chili powder, turmeric, ground coriander, fennel seeds, garam masala and half of the cumin and cook over low heat, squashing the tomato under the back of a wooden spoon to make a thick paste.

4   Drain and add the vegetables with about 4 tbsp water. Cover and cook for 15 minutes, until the potato is tender but not soft.

5   Meanwhile, heat the remaining butter or ghee in a separate saucepan and add the remaining cumin. Add to the curry with the remaining cilantro leaves and salt to taste.

Cauliflower with Coconut and Spices
(Narial Phul Gobi Masala)

Serves 4
75 g (3 oz) potato
450 g (1 lb) cauliflower
100 g (4 oz) grated coconut
1 green chili
15 g (½ oz) fresh ginger, finely grated
1 clove garlic, finely chopped
leaves from 1 sprig of cilantro
½ tsp turmeric
1 small onion, finely chopped
4 cashew nuts
2 tbsp oil
1 tsp mustard seeds
4–6 curry leaves
1 red chili, cut into 4 pieces
75 g (3 oz) tomatoes, chopped
2 tsp lemon juice
salt

1 Peel the potato and cut into chunks. Divide the cauliflower into florets, discarding the tough stalks. Put the vegetables in a saucepan of cold water to prevent discoloration.

2 In a blender, coarsely blend the coconut, green chili, ginger, garlic, cilantro leaves, turmeric, onion and cashew nuts.

3 Drain the vegetables, stir them in the spice mixture to coat and leave for about 10 minutes to absorb the flavors.

4 Heat the oil in a saucepan and when hot, add the mustard seeds, half of the curry leaves and the red chili. Leave them to sizzle for a few seconds until all the seeds have popped.

5 Add the spiced vegetables and tomatoes to the pan, cover and cook on low heat, stirring occasionally, for about 10 minutes, until the potato is tender but not soft.

6 Sprinkle over the lemon juice, stir in the remaining curry leaves and add salt to taste.

Green Beans and Potato Toran
(Aloo Han Moong Toran)

Serves 2
50–75 g (2–3 oz) butter or ghee (see page 16)
1 small onion, finely chopped
225 g (8 oz) tomatoes, peeled and finely chopped
½ tsp garam masala (see page 17)
½ tsp turmeric
½ tsp chili powder
225 g (8 oz) green beans, trimmed and cut into 2.5 cm (1 in) lengths
225 g (8 oz) potatoes, peeled and diced
1 green chili, cut into pieces
15 g (½ oz) fresh ginger, finely grated
1 clove garlic, finely chopped
leaves from 1 sprig of cilantro
salt

1 Heat the butter or ghee in a large saucepan and fry the onion until golden.

2 Add the tomato, stir well and squash it with the back of a wooden spoon until it forms a paste.

3 Add the garam masala, turmeric and chili powder and continue to fry, stirring, for about 5 minutes.

4 Add the beans, potatoes, green chili, ginger, garlic and cilantro leaves with 1 tbsp water and cook gently over low heat, with the lid tightly on, stirring occasionally, for 10–15 minutes, until the vegetables are done. Add salt to taste.

Mushroom with Potatoes and Onions
(Khumbi, Aloo Aur Pyaz)

Serves 2

5 tbsp oil

1 large potato, diced into 2 cm (¾ in) pieces

4 green cardamom pods

4 cm (1½ in) cinnamon stick

2 bay leaves

1 large onion, finely sliced

2 cloves garlic, crushed

2 cm (¾ in) ginger, grated

1 tsp ground turmeric

½ tsp chili powder

½ tsp salt

big pinch of sugar

1½ tsp white vinegar

225 g (8 oz) mushrooms, quartered

1 Heat the oil in a karai over medium high heat. Add the potatoes and fry for 2–3 minutes until light golden in color. Remove the potatoes and set aside.

2 To the same oil add the cardamom pods, cinnamon and bay leaves and let them sizzle for a few seconds.

3 Add the onions, garlic and ginger and fry for 4–5 minutes until soft and golden.

4 Add the turmeric, chili powder, salt, sugar and vinegar and fry, stirring continuously, for another minute.

5 Add the mushrooms and potatoes to the spice mixture and mix thoroughly.

6 Lower the heat to medium, cover and cook for about 15 minutes until the potatoes are tender.

Roasted Cauliflower
(Baked Gobi)

Serves 2
4 medium tomatoes
1 large onion
3 cloves garlic
1 cm (½ in) ginger
2 tbsp ghee (see page 16)
¾ tsp ground turmeric
½ tsp chili powder
½ tsp garam masala (see page 17)
175 g (6 oz) peas
½ tsp salt
1 medium-sized cauliflower, blanched

1 Blend the tomatoes, onion, garlic, and ginger in a blender until you have a paste.
2 Heat the ghee in a frying pan over medium heat and add the paste, turmeric, chili, and garam masala and stirfry until the ghee and spices separate, about 5–6 minutes.
3 Add the peas and salt and cook for 5 more minutes, stirring constantly. Remove from the heat.
4 Chop the cauliflower and place in a large ovenproof dish and pour the spices over it. Place in a preheated oven at 190°C/375°F/Gas Mark 5 for 30–35 minutes. Serve on a flat plate with the peas and spices poured over.

Cauliflower with Coconut Milk
(Narial Phul Gobi)

Serves 4
flesh of 1 coconut, grated
450 g (1 lb) cauliflower, cut into florets, tough stalks discarded
100 g (4 oz) potatoes, peeled and cubed
15 g (½ oz) fresh ginger, finely grated
½ tsp turmeric
½ tsp sambar powder (see page 11)
1 small onion, finely chopped
1 green chili, sliced
4–6 curry leaves
2–3 tbsp oil
1 tsp mustard seeds
salt
leaves from 1 sprig of cilantro

1 Purée the coconut in a blender with 1 tbsp boiling water. Transfer to a sheet of muslin and squeeze the milk into a bowl. Return the coconut to the blender and repeat the process.
2 Simmer the cauliflower and potato in the coconut milk with the ginger, turmeric, sambar powder, three-quarters of the onion and the chili for about 12 minutes, until the vegetables are tender but not soft. Add the curry leaves.
3 Meanwhile, heat the oil in a saucepan and when hot, add the mustard seeds. Let them sizzle for a few seconds until they have all popped.
4 Add the remaining onion and fry until golden, then add to the curry.
5 Add salt to taste and garnish with cilantro.

Cauliflower and Potato Curry
(Aloo Gobi Dalna)

Serves 4
6 tbsp oil
450 g (1 lb) potatoes, peeled and quartered
1 small cauliflower, cut into large florets
pinch of asafetida
¾ tsp ground turmeric
½ tsp chili powder
1½ tsp ground cumin
¾ tsp salt
big pinch of sugar
2 tomatoes, chopped
300 ml (10 fl oz) water
2 tsp ghee (see page 16)
½ tsp garam masala (see page 17)

1. Heat the oil in a karai over medium high heat.
2. Fry the potatoes a few pieces at a time until slightly brown. Remove and set aside.
3. Fry the cauliflower pieces a few at a time until brown spots appear on them. Remove and set aside.
4. Lower the heat to medium, add the asafetida and after 3–4 seconds add the turmeric, chili, cumin, salt and sugar. Mix the spices together, add the tomatoes and fry for 1 minute with the spices.
5. Add the water and bring to a boil. Put in the potatoes, cover and cook for 10 minutes.
6. Add the cauliflower, cover again and cook for 5–7 more minutes until the potatoes and cauliflower are tender.
7. Add the ghee and sprinkle with the garam masala and chopped fresh cilantro. Remove from the heat and serve hot with rice and red lentils.

Cauliflower with Potatoes and Peas
(Aloo Gobi Aur Mater)

Serves 4

4 tbsp oil

2 medium onions, finely chopped

450 g (1 lb) potatoes, diced into 2 cm (¾ in) pieces

1 small cauliflower, cut into 2 cm (¾ in) pieces

½ tsp ground turmeric

½ tsp chili powder

1 tsp ground cumin

2 tomatoes, chopped

1 tsp salt

¼ tsp sugar

200 g (7 oz) peas

½ tsp garam masala (see page 17)

1 Heat the oil in a karai over medium high heat.

2 Add the onions and fry for 3–4 minutes until light brown.

3 Add the potatoes and cauliflower and stir. Add the turmeric, chilli, cumin, tomatoes, salt and sugar. Stirfry for 2–3 minutes.

4 Add the peas, cover and reduce heat to medium low and cook for about 20 minutes until the potatoes and cauliflower are tender. While cooking, stir the vegetables a few times to stop them from sticking.

5 Sprinkle with garam masala before serving.

Pumpkin with Spices
(Masala Kaddu)

Serves 2

2 tbsp oil
½ tsp nigella seeds
2 dried red chilies
1 large onion, finely sliced
450 g (1 lb) pumpkin, diced into 1 cm
   (½ in) cubes
½ tsp ground turmeric
½ tsp chili powder
½ tsp salt

1 Heat oil in a karai over medium high heat, add the nigella seeds and red chilies and let them sizzle for about 15 seconds. Add the onions and fry until golden.
2 Add the pumpkin, turmeric, chili and salt and stirfry for 2–3 minutes. Cover, lower heat to medium and cook for 10 more minutes. Serve hot with Lucchi (see page 108).

Pumpkin and Potato
(Aloo Pethi)

Serves 2

1 tbsp sambar powder (see page 11)
225 g (8 oz) unripe pumpkin, peeled
   and cubed
100 g (4 oz) potato, peeled and cubed
2 tbsp oil
½ tsp mustard seeds
1 small onion, chopped
4–6 curry leaves
¼ tsp asafetida
½ tsp turmeric
1 red chili
100 g (4 oz) tomatoes, peeled and chopped
salt

1 Sprinkle the sambar powder over the pumpkin and potato. Stir well to coat and set aside.
2 Heat the oil in a saucepan and add the mustard seeds. Let them sizzle for a few seconds until they have all popped, then add the onions, curry leaves, asafetida, turmeric and red chili. Stir well and fry until the onion is golden.
3 Add the marinated vegetables, the tomato and enough water to just cover, and simmer for about 15 minutes over low heat, until the vegetables are tender but not soft and the sauce is thick. Add salt to taste.

Eggplant and Potato Toran
(Baigan Aloo Toran)

Serves 4

300 g (10 oz) small eggplants
225 g (8 oz) potatoes
15 g (½ oz) fresh ginger, finely grated
2 cloves garlic, chopped
leaves from 1 sprig of cilantro
1 tsp ground coriander
½ tsp chili powder
½ tsp garam masala
½ tsp turmeric
juice from 25–50 g (1–2 oz) seedless tamarind
1 small onion, finely chopped
2 tbsp oil
salt

1 Cut the eggplants into large chunks, peel and cube the potatoes and leave in a saucepan of cold water to prevent discoloration while you prepare the spices.
2 In a blender, blend together the ginger, garlic, cilantro leaves, powdered spices, tamarind juice and onion.
3 Heat the oil in a saucepan and add the blended spices. Stir-fry for 3–4 minutes, until the oil runs clear of the spices.
4 Drain the vegetables, add them to the saucepan and cook, tightly covered, over low heat for 15–20 minutes, until tender. Add 1–2 tbsp water if necessary, and stir occasionally to prevent the vegetables from sticking.
5 Add salt to taste.

Spicy Eggplant
(Baigan Bharta)

Serves 2

450 g (1 lb) eggplants
3 tbsp oil
1 large onion, finely chopped
3 tomatoes, chopped
1 tbsp cilantro leaves, chopped
1–2 green chilies, chopped
½ tsp ground turmeric
½ tsp chili powder
¾ tsp ground coriander
¾ tsp salt
handful of cooked peas

1 Broil the eggplants for about 15 minutes, turning frequently until the skin turns black and the flesh is soft. Peel off the skin and mash the flesh.
2 Heat the oil in a karai over medium heat and fry the onions until soft. Add the tomatoes, cilantro leaves and green chilies and fry another 2–3 minutes.
3 Add the mashed eggplant, turmeric, chili, cilantro and salt and stir.
4 Fry for another 10–12 minutes and serve with Chappatis (see page 106). Garnish with peas.

Okra Curry
(Bhindi Curry)

Serves 2
225 g (8 oz) okra
3 tbsp oil
grated flesh of ½ coconut
½ tsp chili powder
½ tsp turmeric
½ tsp ground cumin
225 g (8 oz) yogurt
½ tsp mustard seeds
1 red chili, cut into pieces
leaves from 1 sprig of cilantro, chopped
4–6 curry leaves
salt

1 Wash the okra and dry them on paper towels. Cut into 2.5 cm (1 in) lengths.
2 Heat 1 tbsp oil and fry the okra for about 2 minutes, turning gently, until all the oil has been absorbed. Remove with a slotted spoon and set aside.
3 Blend the coconut with the chili powder, turmeric and cumin in a blender, adding 1 tbsp water to make a smooth paste. Mix this into the yogurt.
4 Heat the remaining oil and when hot, add the mustard seeds and red chili. Let them sizzle for a few seconds, until all the seeds have popped, then add the okra.
5 Turn the heat down and add the yogurt mix. Cook gently for 2–3 minutes, stirring to prevent the yogurt from separating, until heated through. Add the cilantro and curry leaves, and salt to taste.

Masala Eggplant
(Tel Baigan)

Serves 2
1 large eggplant, cut into large pieces
½ tsp salt
big pinch of turmeric
8 tbsp mustard oil
½ tsp nigella seeds
¾ tsp ground turmeric
½ tsp chili powder
½ tsp salt
¼ tsp sugar
4 tbsp yogurt
50 ml (2 fl oz) water
2–3 green chilies
1 tsp ground roast cumin seeds (see page 18)

1 Rub the eggplant pieces with the ½ tsp salt and a big pinch of turmeric and set aside for 30 minutes.
2 Heat the oil in a karai over high heat and fry the eggplant until brown. Drain on paper towels.
3 Lower the heat to medium and add the nigella seeds. After 4–5 seconds add the turmeric, chili powder, salt, sugar and yogurt. Stir-fry for 1 minute.
4 Add the water; when it starts to boil add the eggplants and green chilies and cook for 5 minutes.
5 Before removing from the heat, sprinkle with the roast ground cumin. Serve with rice.

Fried Okra with Onions
(Bhindi Bhaji)

Serves 2–3
450 g (1 lb) okra
3 tbsp oil
2 large onions, finely chopped
1 tsp salt

1 Wash the okra and pat dry with paper towels.
2 Cut into 1 cm (½ in) pieces.
3 Heat the oil in a karai over medium heat and fry the onions until soft.
4 Add the okra and salt, and, stirring gently, continue frying until the okra is cooked, about 10–12 minutes. Serve with rice and legumes or Paratha (see page 107).

Okra Toran
(Bhindi Toran)

Serves 2
300 g (10 oz) okra
3 tbsp oil
½ tsp mustard seeds
1 tsp polished split black lentils (urid dal)
1 small onion, chopped
15 g (½ oz) fresh ginger, finely grated
2 green chilies, chopped
25–50 g (1–2 oz) grated or dried coconut
4–6 curry leaves
salt

1 Wash the okra and dry on paper towels. Cut into 2 cm (¾ in) lengths.
2 Seal the okra by frying in 2 tbsp oil, turning frequently, until all the oil is absorbed. Remove the okra from the saucepan and set aside.
3 Add the remaining oil to the saucepan and when hot, add the mustard seeds and dal. Let them sizzle for a few seconds until all the mustard seeds have popped and the dal is golden, then add the onion and fry until golden.
4 Add the ginger and green chili and continue to fry for 3–4 minutes. Stir in the coconut and curry leaves. Add salt to taste.

Fried Spiced Okra
(Bhindi Masala)

Serves 2
225 g (8 oz) okra
50 g (2 oz) butter or ghee (see page 16)
1 small onion, finely chopped
1 clove garlic, finely chopped
1 green chili, chopped
15 g (½ oz) fresh ginger
finely chopped leaves from 1 sprig of cilantro
100 g (4 oz) tomatoes, peeled and
    roughly chopped
½ tsp ground coriander
½ tsp turmeric
½ tsp chili powder
1 tsp garam masala (see page 17)
salt

1   Wash the okra and dry them on paper towels. Cut into 2.5 cm (1 in) lengths. Heat half of the butter or ghee in a pan, add the okra and fry gently. Keep turning them so that they are cooked on all sides, until most of the fat has been absorbed (about 2 minutes). Remove with a slotted spoon and set aside.
2   Add the remaining butter or ghee to the saucepan and when hot, add the onion, garlic, green chili, ginger and cilantro leaves. Stir-fry until the onion is golden.
3   Add the tomato, ground coriander, turmeric, chili powder and garam masala and continue to cook, mashing the tomato under the back of a wooden spoon to make a paste.
4   When the butter runs clear of the spices, add the okra and cook on low heat, stirring occasionally, for about 10 minutes. Add salt to taste.

Okra with Yogurt
(Dahi Bhindi)

Serves 2–3
450 g (1 lb) okra
4 tbsp oil
½ tsp panch phoron
1 cm (½ in) ginger, grated
2 green chilies, cut lengthways
big pinch of turmeric
½ tsp salt
150 ml (5 fl oz) yogurt
8–10 curry leaves

1   Wash the okra and pat dry on paper towels. Cut into 2.5 cm (1 in) pieces.
2   Heat the oil in a karai over medium high heat, add the panch phoron, ginger and chilies. Let them sizzle for a few seconds.
3   Add the okra and, stirring gently, fry for 5 minutes. Lower the heat to medium low.
4   Add the turmeric, salt and yogurt and mix gently with the okra. Cover and cook for 10 minutes.
5   Add the curry leaves and cook for 5 more minutes. Serve with rice or Poori (see page 112).

Stuffed Bitter Gourds
(Sabu Karela)

Serves 4
450 g (1 lb) bitter gourds
1 tsp salt
1 tsp chili powder
2 tbsp mango powder (amchur)
4 tbsp oil

1 Scrape the gourds and slit them lengthways from the tip, leaving the two halves joined at the stalk. Sprinkle salt inside and out and leave the gourds in a cool place for 15 minutes.
2 Scrape away the seeds and squeeze the gourds to remove the moisture drawn from them by the salt.
3 Mix together the chili powder, mango powder and remaining salt.
4 Sprinkle the insides of the gourds with oil and stuff the spice mixture inside. Tie the gourds together with thread.
5 Heat the remaining oil over low heat and fry the gourds, turning gently for 5–10 minutes, until cooked. Remove the thread.
6 Serve hot or cold.

Bitter Gourds with Onion Stuffing
(Piyaz Karela)

Serves 2
225 g (8 oz) bitter gourds
salt
1 onion, finely chopped
1 tsp chili powder
15 g (½ oz) fresh ginger, finely grated
2 tbsp lemon juice
4 tbsp oil

1 Scrape the gourds and slit them lengthways from the tip, leaving the two halves joined at the stalk. Sprinkle salt inside and out and leave the gourds in a cool place for 15 minutes.
2 Scrape away the seeds and squeeze the gourds to remove the moisture drawn from them by the salt.
3 In a blender, purée the onion, chili, 1 tsp salt and the ginger, then mix in the lemon juice.
4 Stuff the gourds with the onion mixture and tie them together with thread. Leave to stand for 5–10 minutes.
5 Heat the oil in a pan, add the gourds and fry over low heat, turning gently, for 5–10 minutes, until done. Remove the thread and serve.

MEAT AND POULTRY

Goat is the meat most often eaten in India, and lamb is the best substitute. Shoulder or neck are the best cuts to buy as they have more connective tissue. This means that they can be cooked for a fairly long time and end up succulent and tender. All recipes in this section are intended for de-boned meat, but the bones can be left in. If you wish to do this, allow for the weight of the bones, which will be about half the total weight of the meat. Beef and pork may also be used, although beef is not often eaten in India. For Hindus, the cow is a sacred animal, and Muslims are forbidden to eat pork.

Meat and Vegetable Curry
(Sabzi Gosht)

Serves 4

75 g (3 oz) butter or ghee (see page 16)
1 small onion, finely chopped
5 g (½ oz) fresh ginger, grated
2 cloves garlic, chopped
½ tsp turmeric
½ tsp chili powder
½ tsp ground coriander
½ tsp garam masala (see page 17)
½ tsp ground cumin
1 green chili, chopped
4–6 curry leaves
450 g (1 lb) meat, trimmed and cubed
175 g (6 oz) tomatoes, peeled and chopped
100 g (4 oz) okra, trimmed and cut into
  2 or 3 pieces
100 g (4 oz) carrots, peeled and diced
225 g (8 oz) potatoes, peeled and cubed
175 g (6 oz) eggplant, peeled and cubed
50 g (2 oz) fresh peas
salt

1 Heat the butter or ghee in a pan, add the onion and fry until golden.
2 Add the ginger, garlic, turmeric, chili powder, cilantro, garam masala, cumin, green chili and curry leaves, stir and fry for 5 more minutes.
3 Add the meat and fry for 5 minutes, then add the tomato, okra, carrot, potato, eggplant and peas, pour on 900 ml (2 pts) water, add ½ tsp salt and cook over low heat for 1 hour, until the vegetables and meat are tender and the sauce is thick.
4 Add extra salt to taste.

Meat Kebabs
(Seekh Kebabs)

Serves 4

5 g (½ oz) fresh ginger, finely grated
1 green chili, chopped
salt
½ tsp garam masala (see page 17)
450 g (1 lb) lean ground meat
1 onion, finely chopped
½ tsp chili powder
½ tsp ground pepper
½ tsp ground cumin
leaves from 1 sprig of cilantro
1 egg, beaten
6 tbsp oil

1 Grind, pound or purée in a blender the ginger, green chili, ½ tsp salt and the garam masala with 1–2 tbsp water to make a paste.
2 In a bowl, mix the spice paste with the meat and onion, sprinkle on the chili powder, pepper, cumin and cilantro leaves, add the egg and 1–2 tsp oil and combine well.
3 Roll the mixture into small sausages and thread onto skewers.
4 Grill the kebabs for 20 minutes, basting with a little oil, and turning frequently until cooked through.
5 Remove the kebabs from the skewers and fry in the remaining oil for about 10 minutes, turning gently.

Pork Vindaloo
(Soor Vindaloo)

Serves 4

6 cloves garlic
25 g (1 oz) fresh ginger
4 red chilies, seeded
1 tsp mustard seeds
½ tsp fenugreek seeds
½ tsp turmeric
½ tsp ground cumin
4 tbsp white wine vinegar
2–3 tbsp oil
2 onions, finely chopped
225 g (8 oz) tomatoes, peeled and chopped
1–1.4 kg (2–3 lb) of shoulder of pork, trimmed
    and cubed
salt
600 ml (1 pt) boiling water
4–6 curry leaves
6 cloves
2.5 cm (1 in) cinnamon stick
1 tsp sugar

1 Chop 4 cloves garlic with half of the ginger, then grind, pound or purée in a blender with the chilies, mustard seeds, fenugreek seeds, turmeric, cumin and half of the vinegar.
2 Heat the oil, add the onion and fry until golden.
3 Add the spice paste, stir and fry gently for 15 minutes.
4 Add the tomato and continue to cook, mashing it under the back of a wooden spoon to make a paste.
5 When the oil has run clear of the spices, add the pork and fry for 5 minutes, turning the pieces in the spice mixture.
6 Add ½ tsp salt and pour on the boiling water. Simmer, covered, for 40 minutes, until the pork is tender.
7 Slice the remaining garlic and ginger and add with the curry leaves, cloves and cinnamon stick. Cook for 5 more minutes.
8 Add the sugar and remaining vinegar. Add salt to taste.

Chicken Curry with Nuts and Coconut Milk
(Narial Gosht)

Serves 4

flesh of 1 coconut, grated
50 g (2 oz) cashew nuts
2 cloves garlic, chopped
½ tsp chili powder
5 g (½ oz) fresh ginger, grated
½ tsp ground coriander
½ tsp turmeric
leaves from 1 sprig of cilantro
½ tsp garam masala (see page 17)
½ tsp ground pepper
100 g (4 oz) butter or ghee (see page 16)
1 small onion, chopped
1 kg (2 lb 3 oz) chicken, trimmed and cubed
¼ tsp saffron
25 g (1 oz) golden raisins
50 g (2 oz) almonds
salt
4–6 curry leaves

1. Purée the coconut in a blender with 1 tbsp boiling water. Transfer to a sheet of muslin and squeeze out the milk into a bowl. Return the coconut to the blender and repeat the process.
2. Grind, pound or purée in a blender the cashew nuts, garlic, chili powder, ginger, ground coriander, turmeric, cilantro leaves, garam masala and pepper.
3. Heat the butter or ghee in a pan, add the onion and fry until golden, then add the blended spices and fry for 5 more minutes.
4. Add the chicken, stir and fry for 5 minutes, then pour on the coconut milk; add the saffron, raisins, almonds and ½ tsp salt and cook, covered, over low heat for about 1 hour, until the chicken is tender and the sauce has thickened.
5. Sprinkle on the curry leaves.

Meatball and Cauliflower Curry
(Phul Gobi Kofta)

Serves 4

1 egg, beaten
450 g (1 lb) lean
  ground meat
15 g (½ oz) fresh
  ginger, grated
2 cloves garlic,
  chopped
½ tsp garam masala
½ tsp ground cumin
leaves from 1 sprig
  of cilantro
salt
small cauliflower, cut
  into florets, tough
  stalks discarded

Sauce

75 g (3 oz) butter
  or ghee
1 small onion,
  finely chopped

cardamom seeds from
  2 pods, crushed
2 cloves
2.5 cm (1 in)
  cinnamon stick
5 g (½ oz) fresh
  ginger, grated
2 cloves garlic,
  crushed
½ tsp turmeric
1 tsp chili powder
½ tsp ground cumin
½ tsp ground
  coriander
225 g (8 oz) tomatoes,
  peeled and
  chopped or 2 tbsp
  tomato paste
150 ml (4 oz) yogurt
salt
leaves from 1 sprig
  of cilantro

1. Mix the egg with the meat.
2. Grind, pound or purée in a blender the ginger, garlic, garam masala, cumin, cilantro leaves and ½ tsp salt.
3. Mix the spice paste with the meat, form it into small balls and set aside.
4. To make the sauce, heat the butter or ghee in a pan, add the onion and fry until golden.
5. Add the cardamom seeds, cloves, cinnamon, ginger, garlic, turmeric, chili powder, cumin and cilantro and fry for 3–4 minutes, stirring.
6. Add the tomato or tomato paste and cook, stirring, until the fat runs clear of the spices.
7. Stir in the yogurt with a pinch of salt and 1–2 tbsp water and bring gently to a boil.
8. Carefully slide in the meatballs and cauliflower florets and cook for about 20 minutes on low heat, stirring occasionally and being careful not to break the meatballs.
9. Sprinkle on the chopped cilantro leaves and add salt to taste.

Sweet and Sour Lamb Curry
(Chuteraney)

Serves 4

2 tbsp oil	½ tsp garam masala
50 g (2 oz) butter or ghee	½ tsp turmeric
	1 tsp chili powder
2 onions, finely chopped	1 kg (2 lb 3 oz) lamb, trimmed and cubed
1 green chili, chopped	600 ml (1 pt) boiling water
15 g (1 oz) fresh ginger, finely grated	225 g (8 oz) potatoes, peeled and chopped
2 cloves garlic, crushed	½ tsp ground pepper
225 g (8 oz) tomatoes, peeled and chopped	1 tbsp sugar
	150 ml (¼ pt) yogurt
leaves from 2 sprigs of cilantro	2 tbsp lemon juice
	salt

1 Heat the oil and butter or ghee in a pan, add the onion, green chili, ginger and garlic and fry until the onion turns golden.

2 Add the tomato, half of the cilantro leaves, the garam masala, turmeric and chili powder and cook, stirring and squashing the tomato under the back of a wooden spoon until it makes a paste and the fat has run clear of the spices.

3 Add the lamb and boiling water and cook over low heat for about 1 hour, until tender.

4 Add the potato and cook for 10–15 more minutes until tender but not soft.

5 Mix the remaining cilantro leaves, the pepper and sugar with the yogurt, add to the curry and cook for 2–3 minutes, stirring, to heat through.

6 Sprinkle on the lemon juice and chili powder and add salt to taste.

Lamb Curry with Roast Spices
(Masala Gosht)

Serves 4

3 tbsp oil
2 tbsp cilantro seeds
2 red chilies, cut into pieces
2.5 cm (1 in) cinnamon stick
3 cloves
50 g (2 oz) grated coconut
450 g (1 lb) lamb, trimmed and cubed
½ tsp turmeric
salt
2 green chilies, sliced
15 g (½ oz) fresh ginger, grated
1 small onion, chopped
225 g (8 oz) potatoes, peeled and diced
225 g (8 oz) tomatoes, peeled and chopped
900 ml (2 pts) boiling water
6 mint leaves
flaked almonds (optional garnish)
red chili (optional garnish)

1 Heat half of the oil in a saucepan and fry the cilantro seeds, red chili, cinnamon, cloves and coconut for about 5 minutes, then transfer to a grinder or a mortar and reduce into a smooth paste.

2 Put the lamb in a bowl with the turmeric, ½ tsp salt, green chili, ginger and half of the onion, add the spice paste and mix well. Leave to marinate for 15 minutes.

3 Heat the remaining oil in a large saucepan and fry the remaining onion until golden.

4 Add the marinated lamb, the potato and tomato, pour on the boiling water, cover and cook on low heat for about 1 hour, until the lamb is tender and the sauce is thick.

5 Add extra salt to taste and sprinkle on the mint leaves, flaked almonds and chopped chili.

Plain Beef Curry
(Gosht Curry)

Serves 4

1 kg (2 lb 3 oz) beef, trimmed and cubed
600 ml (1 pt) water
1 tbsp lemon juice
salt
2 tbsp ground coriander
2 tsp chili powder
½ tsp ground pepper
½ tsp ground cumin
½ tsp turmeric
50 g (2 oz) butter or ghee (see page 16)
1 tbsp oil
1 small onion, finely chopped
25 g (1 oz) fresh ginger, chopped
2 cloves garlic, chopped
1 tsp garam masala (see page 17)
4–6 curry leaves

1 Wash the beef thoroughly in hot water. Drain and cook, covered, in the measured amount of water with the lemon juice and a pinch of salt for about an hour or until the beef is tender and most of the liquid has evaporated.
2 Mix the cilantro, chili, pepper, cumin and turmeric with 2 tbsp water to make a smooth paste.
3 Heat the butter or ghee in a saucepan with the oil, add the onion, ginger and garlic and fry until the onion is golden.
4 Add the spice paste and continue to fry for 10 minutes. Add the paste to the cooked beef with ½ tsp salt and cook, covered, on low heat for 10–15 minutes, until the sauce is thick.
5 Sprinkle on the garam masala and the curry leaves and add extra salt to taste.

Beef and Tomato Curry
(Tamatar Gosht)

Serves 4

50 g (2 oz) butter or ghee (see page 16)
1 small onion, finely chopped
15 g (½ oz) fresh ginger, finely grated
3 cloves garlic, finely chopped
225 g (8 oz) tomatoes, peeled and chopped
½ tsp turmeric
2 tsp chili powder
1 tbsp ground coriander
½ tsp ground cumin
salt
1 tsp garam masala (see page 17)
600 ml (1 pt) boiling water
1 kg (2 lb 3 oz) beef, trimmed and cubed
225 g (8 oz) potatoes, peeled and diced
leaves from 1 sprig of cilantro

1 Heat the butter or ghee in a large saucepan, add the onion, ginger and garlic and fry until the onion is golden.
2 Add the tomato, turmeric, chili powder, ground coriander, cumin, ½ tsp salt and garam masala. Stir and continue to fry until the fat runs clear of the spices, then add the boiling water and mix well.
3 Add the beef and cook, covered, over low heat for about 1 hour, until tender and the sauce is thick.
4 Add the potato and a little extra water, if necessary, and cook for 10–15 more minutes until tender but not soft.
5 Sprinkle on the cilantro leaves and extra salt to taste.

Beef Curry in a Thick Sauce
(Gosht Dupiaza)

Serves 4

1 small onion, finely chopped
2 tbsp oil
1 tbsp all-purpose flour
1 kg (2 lb 3 oz) beef, trimmed and cubed
1 tbsp lemon juice
½ tsp ground pepper
salt
900 ml (2 pts) water
50 g (2 oz) butter or ghee (see page 16)
225 g (8 oz) tomatoes, chopped
1 green chili, sliced
leaves from 1 sprig of cilantro
½ tsp garam masala (see page 17)

1   Fry the onion in the oil until golden. Add the flour and continue to fry, stirring, until the flour is colored and has formed a paste.
2   Add the beef, lemon juice, pepper and ½ tsp salt, stir and pour on the water. Bring to a boil and simmer, covered, for about 1 hour, stirring occasionally, until the meat is tender and the sauce is thick.
3   Heat the butter or ghee in a pan, add the tomato and green chili and fry gently, stirring, for 3–4 minutes, then add to the meat.
4   Sprinkle on the cilantro leaves and garam masala.

Meat Curry with Yogurt
(Dahi Gosht)

Serves 4
4–6 tbsp oil
2 onions, roughly chopped
25 g (1 oz) fresh ginger, chopped
2 cloves garlic, chopped
1 green chili, chopped
cardamom seeds from 2 pods
2.5 cm (1 in) cinnamon stick
3 cloves
½ tsp fennel seeds
1 tbsp ground coriander
1 tsp ground cumin
leaves from 2 sprigs cilantro
½ tsp turmeric
1 tsp chili powder
150 ml (4 fl oz) yogurt
1 kg (2 lb 3 oz) meat, trimmed and cubed
600 ml (1 pt) boiling water
4–6 curry leaves
salt

1 Heat half of the oil in a pan, add half of the onion, the ginger, garlic, green chili, cardamom seeds, cinnamon, cloves, fennel seeds, ground coriander, cumin, half of the cilantro leaves, the turmeric and chili and fry gently, stirring, for 10 minutes.
2 Take the saucepan off the heat and stir in the yogurt. Mix well and set aside.
3 Chop the remaining onion finely and fry in the remaining oil until golden. Add the cubed meat and fry for about 15 minutes, stirring occasionally.
4 Stir in the spiced yogurt and cook gently for 8–10 minutes, stirring.
5 Pour on the boiling water, turn down the heat and cook, covered, for about 1 hour or until the meat is tender. Cook uncovered if a thicker sauce is required and stir frequently.
6 Sprinkle on the curry leaves and remaining cilantro leaves and salt to taste.

Fried Spiced Beef Keema
(Keema Masala)

Serves 4
100 g (4 oz) butter or ghee (see page 16)
1 onion, finely chopped
2 cloves garlic, finely chopped
15 g (½ oz) fresh ginger, finely grated
leaves from 1 sprig of cilantro
75 g (3 oz) tomatoes, peeled and chopped
cardamom seeds from 2 pods, crushed
2.5 cm (1 in) cinnamon stick
3 cloves
1 bay leaf
½ tsp ground coriander
½ tsp turmeric
½ tsp ground cumin
½ tsp chili powder
salt
1 kg (2 lb 3 oz) beef
225 g (8 oz) potatoes, peeled and diced
300 ml (10 fl oz) boiling water
50 g (2 oz) peas (fresh or frozen)

1 Heat the butter or ghee in a pan, add the onion and fry until golden.
2 Add the garlic, ginger, half of the cilantro leaves, the tomato, cardamom, cinnamon, cloves and bay leaf and fry for 3–4 minutes, stirring.
3 Add the cilantro, turmeric, cumin, chili powder and ½ tsp salt and stir to make a thick paste.
4 Add the beef and potato and fry for about 15 minutes, stirring occasionally, then pour on the boiling water, cover and cook on low heat for 15 minutes, until the beef and potato are cooked and the sauce is thick. Add the peas and cook for a further couple of minutes.
5 Add salt to taste and sprinkle on the remaining cilantro leaves.

Lamb with Cardamom
(Elaichi Gosht)

Serves 4–6
30 black peppercorns
cardamom seeds from 25 pods
5 medium tomatoes
2.5 cm (1 in) ginger, cut into small pieces
120 ml (4 fl oz) oil
2 large onions, finely chopped
1 kg (2 lb 3oz) lamb, cut into 2.5 cm (1 in) cubes
2 tsp paprika
1½ tsp salt
250 ml (8 fl oz) water
3 tbsp cilantro leaves, chopped

1   Grind the peppercorns and cardamom seeds finely.
2   In a blender or food processor, purée the tomatoes and ginger.
3   Heat the oil in a saucepan and fry the onions until golden. Add the meat and the ground spices. Stir constantly and fry for 5 minutes.
4   Add the blended mixture, paprika and salt, mix with the meat and fry for 2–3 more minutes.
5   Add the water, bring it to the boil, cover, lower the heat to very low and cook for about 1 hour until tender. Garnish with cilantro leaves and serve with rice.

Lamb Chop Kebabs
(Bara Kabob)

Serves 4
700 g (1½ lb) lamb chops
475 ml (1 pt) yogurt
1½ tsp salt
2.5 cm (1 in) ginger, grated
8 cloves garlic, crushed
¾ tsp garam masala (see page 17)
1 tbsp poppy seeds, ground
2–3 green chilies, ground
2 tbsp oil

1   Remove excess fat from the chops. Wash and pat dry.
2   Lightly beat the yogurt and mix in all the ingredients.
3   Add the lamb chops and marinate for at least 6 hours. It is best to marinate for 24 hours – if you are going to marinate for this long, cover and refrigerate the meat but make sure it is returned to room temperature before it is grilled.
4   Preheat the grill.
5   Take the chops out of the marinade and place on a baking sheet. Grill for 8–10 minutes on each side.

Chicken Curry with Yogurt
(Murghi Dahi)

Serves 4

4 tbsp oil
2 onions, finely chopped
2 cloves garlic, finely chopped
15 g (½ oz) fresh ginger, finely grated
cardamom seeds from 2 pods
2.5 cm (1 in) cinnamon stick
2 cloves
½ tsp fennel seeds
1 tsp paprika
2 tsp ground coriander
½ tsp ground cumin
½ tsp chili powder
½ tsp turmeric
50 ml (1 ½ oz) yogurt
1.4 kg (3 lb) chicken, skinned and jointed
225 g (8 oz) sweet potatoes, peeled and diced
225 g (8 oz) tomatoes, peeled and chopped
salt
900 ml (2 pts) boiling water
leaves from 2 sprigs of cilantro

1 Heat 3 tbsp oil in a pan, add the onion, garlic, ginger, cardamom seeds, cinnamon, cloves and fennel seeds and fry until the onion is golden.
2 Add the paprika, cilantro, cumin, chili powder and turmeric and continue to fry until the oil runs clear from the spice mixture.
3 Drain off the oil, stir in the yogurt and purée in a blender until smooth.
4 Fry the rest of the onion in the remaining oil until golden, add the chicken and continue to fry for 5 minutes.
5 Add the blended spice mixture, the sweet potato, tomato, ½ tsp salt and boiling water and cook on low heat for about 1 hour, until the meat and vegetables are done.
6 Add extra salt to taste and if you wish to sprinkle cilantro leaves on top.

Spiced Chicken
(Murghi Masala)

Serves 4

3 tbsp cilantro seeds
2 red chilies, cut into 3 or 4 pieces
2.5 cm (1 in) cinnamon stick
2 cloves
50 g (2 oz) grated coconut
½ tsp turmeric
2 onions, finely chopped
15 g (½ oz) fresh ginger, finely grated
4–6 curry leaves
1 kg (2 lb 3 oz) chicken joints, skinned
3 tbsp oil
2 green chilies, seeded and cut into 3 or
   4 pieces
2 bay leaves
900 ml (2 pts) water
100 g (4 oz) tomatoes, peeled and chopped
salt

1 Heat a saucepan without any fat or oil until very hot, then add the cilantro seeds, red chili, cinnamon stick and cloves, and roast them for 5–6 minutes, shaking the saucepan to prevent them from burning. Grind or pound the roast spices into a fine powder.
2 Purée the spices and coconut together in a blender.
3 Stir in the turmeric, three-quarters of the onion, the ginger and half of the curry leaves.
4 Smother the chicken with the spice mixture and leave to marinate for 10–15 minutes.
5 Heat the oil in a pan, add the remaining onion, green chili and bay leaves. Fry until the onion is golden.
6 Add the water to the tomato and chicken pieces and cook gently, covered, for an hour, until the chicken is tender and the sauce is thick.
7 Add salt to taste.

Chicken and Tomato Curry
(Tamatar Aur Murghi)

Serves 4

150 g (5 oz) butter or ghee	½ tsp chili powder
2 onions, chopped	½ tsp paprika
3 cloves garlic, crushed	1 tbsp ground coriander
15 g (½ oz) fresh ginger, finely grated	½ tsp fennel seeds
1 green chili, chopped	1 chicken, about 1.4 kg (3 lb), skinned and jointed
cardamom seeds from 2 pods, crushed	900 ml (2 pts) boiling water
3 cloves	225 g (8 oz) potatoes, peeled and diced
2.5 cm (1 in) cinnamon stick	¼ tsp ground pepper
1 bay leaf	¼ tsp saffron
225 g (8 oz) tomatoes, peeled and chopped	salt
½ tsp turmeric	leaves from 2 sprigs of cilantro

1 Heat the butter or ghee in a pan, add the onion, garlic, ginger, green chili, cardamom seeds, cloves, cinnamon and bay leaf and fry until the onion is golden.
2 Add the tomato and continue to cook, squashing it under the back of a wooden spoon to make a paste.
3 Add the turmeric, chili powder, paprika, ground coriander and fennel seeds and fry until the fat runs clear of the spices.
4 Add the chicken pieces and fry for 5 minutes, then pour on the boiling water, add the potato and cook over low heat, covered, for 1 hour, until the chicken and potato are done and the sauce has thickened.
5 Sprinkle on the pepper, saffron, salt and cilantro leaves.

Chicken Biriyani
(Murghi Biriyani)

Serves 4–6

Chicken

1 tbsp biriyani masala (see page 8)
1 green chili
15 g (½ oz) fresh ginger, finely grated
2 cloves garlic, chopped
leaves from 2 sprigs cilantro
1 tbsp chopped mint leaves
50 g (2 oz) cashew nuts
6 tbsp oil
1.4 kg (3 lb) chicken
50 g (2 oz) butter or ghee
1 small onion, chopped
225 g (8 oz) tomatoes, peeled and chopped
salt
600 ml (1 pt) boiling water

Rice

100 g (4 oz) butter or ghee
2 bay leaves
1 small onion, chopped
225 g (8 oz) basmati rice, washed, soaked in water for 20 minutes and drained
600 ml (1 pt) boiling water
10 cashew nuts
50 g (2 oz) golden raisins

1 Pound, grind or purée in a blender the biriyani masala, green chili, ginger, garlic, cilantro leaves, mint and cashews, adding about 2 tbsp water to make a paste.

2 Skin the chicken and cut into 8 pieces. Wash in hot water and dry on paper towels.

3 Heat 4 tbsp oil in a pan, add the chicken and fry for about 10 minutes, turning once. Remove the chicken with a slotted spoon and set aside.

4 Add the remaining oil and the butter or ghee to the saucepan and when hot, add the onion and fry until golden.

5 Add the spice mixture and cook, stirring, until the fat runs clear of the spices.

6 Add the tomato, mashing it with the back of a wooden spoon to make a paste.

7 Add the chicken pieces and salt and pour on the boiling water. Cook for about 1 hour, until the chicken is tender and the sauce has thickened.

8 Meanwhile, for the rice, heat three-quarters of the butter or ghee in a heavy-based saucepan, add the bay leaves and onion and fry until the onion is golden.

9 Pour on the rice and stir well over low heat for about 10 minutes, until the rice is translucent.

10 Add the boiling water, bring back to a boil and cook on low heat, covered, for 8–10 minutes. Drain off the water.

11 Mix the rice, chicken and sauce together in an ovenproof casserole dish, cover with a lid or foil and cook in the oven at 150°C/300°F/Gas Mark 2 for 10–15 minutes, until the rice is completely cooked. This dish should be moist but not too wet.

12 Fry the cashews and raisins briefly in the remaining butter or ghee and sprinkle on top of the curry.

Chicken with Spices
(Murghi Masala)

Serves 4
2–3 tbsp oil
2 cloves garlic, chopped
5 g (½ oz) fresh ginger, finely grated
leaves from 1 sprig of cilantro
½ tsp garam masala (see page 17)
1 tsp ground coriander
1 tsp ground cumin
4 cashew nuts
1 tbsp paprika
1 tsp chili powder
1 tbsp lemon juice
1–2 tsp salt
150 ml (4 oz) yogurt
8 chicken legs

1 In a blender, purée all the ingredients except the chicken and yogurt into a thick paste, then stir in the yogurt and mix thoroughly.
2 Wash the chicken pieces, dry on paper towels and prick all over with a sharp pointed knife.
3 Smother the chicken in the spice paste and marinate for 3 hours.
4 Lay the chicken pieces on a rack in a roasting pan and cook in the oven at 200°C/400°F/Gas Mark 6 for 45 minutes until the chicken is tender.
5 Sprinkle on extra salt to taste.

Chicken with Honey
(Murghi Madh)

Serves 4
15 g (½ oz) fresh ginger, finely grated
2 cloves garlic, crushed
2 tbsp lemon juice
4 tbsp liquid honey
1 tbsp paprika
1 tsp chili powder
1 tbsp cornstarch
½ tsp salt
8 chicken legs
1 tbsp lemon juice
leaves from 1–2 sprigs cilantro

1 Put the ginger and the next seven ingredients in a mortar or a blender and pound or blend well to make a smooth paste.
2 Wash the chicken pieces, dry them on paper towels and prick them all over with a sharp, pointed knife.
3 Rub the spice paste all over the chicken and leave for at least 20 minutes to marinate.
4 Lay the chicken pieces on a rack in a roasting pan and cook in the oven at 200°C/400°F/Gas Mark 6 for 45 minutes until the meat is cooked through.
5 Sprinkle over the lemon juice and garnish with cilantro leaves.

Chicken, Tandoori Style
(Murghi Tandoori)

Serves 4

8 chicken breasts
1–2 tbsp lemon juice
salt
5 g (½ oz) fresh ginger, finely grated
3 cloves garlic, chopped
1 tsp ground coriander
½ tsp ground cumin
1 tsp chili powder
2 tbsp paprika
red food coloring (optional)
1 tsp garam masala (see page 17)
½ tsp ground black pepper
150 ml (4 fl oz) yogurt
1 cucumber, sliced
1 small onion, sliced

1 Skin the chicken breasts, wash thoroughly and dry on paper towels. Slash them with a sharp pointed knife.

2 Rub in the lemon juice and sprinkle with salt.

3 Blend the ginger and garlic in a blender with 1 tbsp water, then mix with the cilantro, cumin, chili powder, paprika, red food coloring, garam masala and pepper and stir into the yogurt.

4 Smother the chicken breast in the spiced yogurt and leave, covered, in the fridge to marinate overnight.

5 Lay the chicken breast on a rack in a roasting pan and cook in the oven at 200°C/400°F/Gas Mark 6 for about 45 minutes, until tender.

6 Sprinkle with extra salt to taste and garnish with cucumber and onion slices.

FISH AND SHELLFISH

There are said to be over 2,000 varieties of fish and shellfish available in India, and they form an important part of the diet, especially for non-meat-eaters. The cold-water fish that swim in the seas around Europe and America are not natives to the warm waters of the Indian Ocean, but they are equally well suited to Indian cooking. The best varieties are the firm-fleshed white fish such as cod, haddock or halibut.

Sardines in a Thick Spicy Sauce
(Machli Curry)

Serves 4
3 tbsp oil
2 tbsp cilantro seeds
3 red chilies, cut into pieces
50–75 g (2–3 oz) grated coconut
1–2 tbsp tamarind juice
1 green chili, chopped
15 g (½ oz) fresh ginger, finely grated
1 onion, finely chopped
¼ tsp turmeric
450 g (1 lb) fresh sardines, cleaned
salt
4–6 curry leaves

1 Heat half of the oil in a pan, add the cilantro seeds and red chili and fry for 3–4 minutes until the fragrance emerges, then grind, pound or blend with the coconut.
2 Return to the saucepan and continue to fry, adding the tamarind, green chili, ginger, half of the onion and the turmeric, for a further 5–7 minutes, until they make a thick paste.
3 Lay the sardines on a plate, smother them in the paste and leave to marinate for 15 minutes.
4 Meanwhile, heat the remaining oil and fry the remaining onion until golden.
5 Add the marinated sardines to the saucepan with 2 tbsp water, cover and cook on low heat for 5–8 minutes, until tender.
6 Add salt to taste and sprinkle on the curry leaves.

Fried Spiced Fish
(Machi Masala)

Serves 2
1 onion, finely chopped
5 g (½ oz) fresh ginger, finely grated
6 curry leaves
salt
¼ tsp turmeric
1 tsp chili powder
4 tbsp oil
450 g (1 lb) white fish, boned, skinned and cubed

1 Pound, grind or blend in a blender the onion, ginger, curry leaves, ½ tsp salt, the turmeric and chili powder to make a thick paste.
2 Spread the paste over the fish and leave to marinate for about 2 hours.
3 Heat the oil in a large saucepan that the fish will fit into in one layer, add the fish and fry for about 10 minutes, until tender.
4 Add extra salt to taste.

Shrimp Biriyani
(Jhinga Biriyani)

Serves 4

Shrimp

1 green chili
15 g (½ oz) fresh
    ginger, grated
1 clove garlic, chopped
50 g (2 oz) grated or
    dried coconut
4 cashew nuts
2 tsp biriyani masala
    (see page 8)
50 g (2 oz) butter
    or ghee
1 small onion,
    chopped
450 g (1 lb) shelled
    shrimp
salt
1 tbsp lemon juice

cashew nuts and
    sultanas, fried in a
    little butter or ghee,
    for decoration

Rice

50 g (2 oz) butter or
    ghee
small onion, chopped
2 bay leaves
225 g (8 oz) basmati
    rice, washed,
    soaked in water
    for 20 minutes
    and drained
salt
100 g (4 oz) fresh peas

1 Grind, pound or blend in a blender the chili, ginger, garlic, coconut, cashews and biriyani masala to make a thick paste.

2 Heat the butter or ghee in a pan, add the onion and fry until golden.

3 Add the blended spice paste and fry for 5–8 more minutes, stirring.

4 Add the shrimp and ½ tsp salt and cook on a low heat for 3–4 minutes, stirring, until the shrimp are heated through and coated in the spice mixture.

5 For the rice, heat the butter or ghee in a pan, add the onion and bay leaves and fry until the onion turns golden.

6 Pour in the rice, stir and fry for about 10 minutes, until translucent.

7 Add 1 tsp salt, the peas and enough water to cover and simmer on low heat for 10–15 minutes, until the rice is almost cooked.

8 Stir the shrimp and rice together in an ovenproof casserole dish, cover with a lid or foil and cook in the oven at 150°C/300°F/Gas Mark 2 for 10–15 minutes.

9 Sprinkle over the lemon juice, cashews and sultanas and add extra salt to taste.

Shrimp Vindaloo
(Jhinga Vindaloo)

Serves 4

½ tsp cumin seeds
25 g (1 oz) fresh
   ginger, finely grated
1–2 cloves garlic,
   finely chopped
1 tsp mustard seeds
3 tbsp oil
2 onions, finely
   chopped
6 curry leaves
100 g (4 oz) tomatoes,
   peeled and
   chopped

2 tsp chili powder
½ tsp turmeric
450 g (1 lb) shelled
   shrimp (or crayfish)
3 tbsp white wine
   vinegar
1 tsp cornstarch
   (optional)
salt
½ tsp sugar (optional)

1 Crush the cumin seeds with the ginger, garlic and mustard seeds.

2 Heat the oil in a pan, add the onion and curry leaves and fry until the onion is golden.

3 Add the tomato, chili powder, turmeric and 1–2 tbsp water and cook, mashing the tomato under the back of a wooden spoon to make a thick paste.

4 Add the crushed spices and continue to fry for 5 minutes, then add the shrimp or crayfish and 4 tbsp water and simmer for 10 minutes.

5 Pour in the vinegar. The sauce may be thickened, if necessary, by adding the cornstarch mixed with 1 tsp water. Add salt to taste and sugar, if desired.

Spiced Shrimp
(Jhinga Batana)

Serves 4

450 g (1 lb) shrimp
1½ tsp salt
½ tsp ground turmeric
4 cloves garlic
2 cm (¾ in) ginger
2 green chilis
6 tbsp oil
2 medium onions, finely chopped
1½ tsp ground coriander
1½ tsp ground cumin
175 ml (6 fl oz) water
175 g (6 oz) peas
1 tsp corn syrup or brown sugar
2 tbsp tamarind juice (see page 16)
2 tbsp chopped cilantro leaves
2 tbsp grated coconut

1 Shell the shrimp, leaving the tails on. Make a small cut along the back to remove the black vein. Wash the shrimp and rub in ½ tsp of the salt and turmeric. Put aside for 1 hour.

2 Grind the garlic, ginger and green chilies into a paste.

3 In a large saucepan, heat the oil and fry the onions until lightly golden.

4 Add the shrimp and paste and stirfry for 2–3 minutes.

5 Add the cilantro, cumin and remaining salt, and continue to fry for one more minute.

6 Add the water, bring to a boil, reduce the heat to medium low, cover and simmer for 10 minutes.

7 Add the peas, corn syrup or sugar and tamarind juice, cover again and cook for about 20 minutes until the shrimp are tender. Garnish with the cilantro leaves and coconut.

Fish Cooked in Coconut Milk
(Mouli)

Serves 4
700 g (1½ lb) white fish, cleaned
50 g (2 oz) creamed coconut
250 ml (8 fl oz) boiling water
4 tbsp oil
3 cloves
1 medium onion, finely chopped
¼ tsp ground turmeric
1 tsp salt
3–4 green chilies
6–8 curry leaves

1   Cut the fish into 8–10 equal-sized pieces.
2   Blend together the creamed coconut and the boiling water in a blender or food processor until smooth.
3   Heat the oil over medium heat and fry the pieces of fish, a few at a time, until lightly browned. Keep on one side.
4   Add the cloves to the remaining oil. When they swell up, add the onion and fry until lightly golden. Add the turmeric and salt and stirfry for a few seconds.
5   Add the fish gently and mix.
6   Add the coconut milk and, when it starts to boil, cover, lower the heat to medium low and cook for about 10–12 minutes.
7   Add the chilies and curry leaves and cook for another couple of minutes until the fish is tender. Serve hot with rice.

Fish in a Yogurt Sauce
(Dahi Mach)

Serves 4
1½ tsp salt
700 g (1½ lb) white fish, cleaned and cut into 2.5 cm (1 in) pieces
4 tbsp ghee (see page 16)
6 green cardamom pods
5 cm (2 in) cinnamon stick
2 bay leaves
1 medium onion, finely sliced
2 cm (¾ in) ginger, grated
1 tbsp raisins
2–3 green chilies
about 120 ml (4 fl oz) plain yogurt
175 ml (6 fl oz) water
½ tsp sugar

1   Sprinkle ½ tsp of salt on the fish and rub into the pieces.
2   Heat the ghee in a karai or saucepan over medium high heat, and gently fry the pieces of fish, a few at a time, until lightly golden. Put aside.
3   In the remaining ghee, add the cardamom, cinnamon and bay leaves and let them sizzle for 3–4 seconds.
4   Add the onion, ginger and raisins and fry, stirring constantly, until the onion is golden.
5   Add the chilies, yogurt, water, sugar and the remaining salt and bring to a boil. Gently add the pieces of fish. Cover, lower the heat and cook for 15–20 minutes until the fish is cooked and the gravy is slightly thickened.

Shrimp in a Coconut Sauce
(Chingre Macher Malai)

Serves 4

450 g (1 lb) shrimp
1½ tsp ground turmeric
1½ tsp salt
50 g (2 oz) creamed coconut
300 ml (10 fl oz) hot water
120 ml (4 fl oz) oil
2 medium potatoes, peeled and quartered
1 large onion, finely sliced
½ tsp chili powder
½ tsp sugar
2–3 green chilies

1 Shell the shrimp, leaving the tails on. Make a small cut along the back to remove the black vein. Wash and pat dry. Rub ½ tsp each of turmeric and salt into the shrimp.

2 In a food processor or blender, blend together the creamed coconut and water. Put aside.

3 Heat the oil in a saucepan and fry the potatoes until evenly browned. Put aside.

4 Add the shrimp and fry until golden. Put aside.

5 Add the onion to the remaining oil and fry until golden brown. Add the remaining turmeric, salt, chili powder and sugar and fry for 1–2 minutes with the onion.

6 Add the blended coconut milk and bring to a boil. Add the shrimp and green chilies.

7 Cover, lower the heat and cook for 10 minutes. Add the potatoes, cover again and cook for 20–25 more minutes, until the shrimp are cooked and the gravy is thickened.

Fish Curry
(Macher Kalia)

Serves 4
700 g (1½ lb) white fish, cleaned
1½ tsp ground turmeric
1½ tsp salt
1 medium onion, quartered
2 cloves garlic
2 cm (¾ in) ginger
1 tbsp vinegar
8 tbsp oil
2 medium potatoes, peeled and quartered
4 green cardamom pods
5 cm (2 in) cinnamon stick, broken in half
2 bay leaves
½ tsp chili powder
¼ tsp sugar
300 ml (10 fl oz) water
3–4 green chilies

1 Cut the fish into 8–10 equal-sized pieces.
2 Rub ½ tsp each of turmeric and salt into the fish.
3 In a food processor or blender, blend together the onion, garlic, ginger and vinegar.
4 Heat the oil in a karai or saucepan and fry the potatoes, turning often, until evenly browned. Put aside.
5 Gently add a few pieces of fish and fry until golden. Put aside.
6 In the remaining oil, add the cardamom, cinnamon and bay leaves and let them sizzle for 5–6 seconds.
7 Add the blended mixture and, stirring constantly, fry until golden brown.
8 Add the remaining turmeric, salt, chili powder and sugar, mix thoroughly with the onion mixture and fry for 1–2 minutes.
9 Add the water and green chilies and bring to a boil. Add the pieces of potato and fish. Cover, lower the heat and cook for 15–20 minutes until the potatoes are tender. Serve with rice.

Fish in a Hot Sauce
(Macher Jhal)

Serves 4
700 g (1½ lb) white fish, cleaned
1½ tsp ground turmeric
1½ tsp salt
120 ml (4 fl oz) oil
1 large onion, finely sliced
½ tsp chili powder
250 ml (8 fl oz) water
2–3 green chilies

1 Cut the fish into 8–10 equal-sized pieces.
2 Rub ½ tsp each of turmeric and salt into the fish.
3 Heat the oil in a karai or saucepan over medium high heat and fry the pieces of fish, a few at a time, until lightly browned. Put aside.
4 In the remaining oil, fry the onion until brown. Add the remaining turmeric, salt and chili powder and stirfry for one more minute.
5 Add the water and bring to the boil; gently add the pieces of fish and the green chilies. Cover, lower the heat to medium and cook for about 15 minutes until the fish is cooked and the gravy is thickened.

Steamed Shrimp
(Bhape Chirigre)

Serves 2
450 g (1 lb) shrimp
1 tsp ground turmeric
½ tsp chili powder
1 tsp black mustard seeds, ground
2–3 green chilies
1 tsp salt
2 tbsp oil

1 Shell the shrimp, leaving the tails on. Make a small cut down the back to remove the black vein. Wash and pat dry.

2 Thoroughly mix all the ingredients with the shrimp. Place the mixture in a bowl (half-fill it only), and secure a double thickness of aluminum foil around the top of the bowl.

3 In a large saucepan, boil some water and place the bowl of shrimp in the saucepan, so that the water reaches a quarter of the way up the bowl.

4 Cover the saucepan, lower the heat and keep boiling, topping up the boiling water during cooking as necessary. Steam for about 30–40 minutes.

EGGS

Eggs can be used to make a very quick and satisfying curry. Hard-boiled eggs can be shelled and pierced with the point of a sharp knife to let in the flavors of the sauce they are being cooked in. Curried scrambled eggs make a very speedy lunch for one, as well as an unusual side dish at dinner.

Egg Curry I
(Andey Ki Curry)

Serves 4–6
3–4 tbsp oil
2 small onions, grated
15 g (½ oz) fresh ginger, grated
2 cloves garlic, crushed
2.5 cm (1 in) cinnamon stick
1 bay leaf
½ tsp chili powder
2 tbsp ground coriander
2 cashew nuts, ground
225 g (8 oz) tomatoes, peeled and chopped
120 ml (4 fl oz) water
salt
6 hard-boiled eggs
½ tsp garam masala (see page 17)
leaves from 1 sprig of cilantro
1 tsp lemon juice
4 peppercorns, crushed

1 Heat the oil in a pan, add the onion, ginger, garlic, cinnamon and bay leaf and fry until the onion is golden.
2 Add the chili powder, ground coriander, cashews and tomato and continue to cook, mashing the tomato under the back of a wooden spoon to make a thick paste.
3 Pour on the water with ½ tsp salt, bring to a boil and add the eggs. Cook over low heat for 5 minutes.
4 Take the curry off the heat and sprinkle on the garam masala, cilantro leaves, lemon juice and pepper. Add extra salt to taste.

Egg Curry II
(Andey Ki Curry)

Serves 4
4 tbsp oil
1 large onion, finely sliced
2 tbsp Onion Mix (see page 17)
½ tsp ground turmeric
½ tsp chili powder
¾ tsp salt
big pinch of sugar
8 hard-boiled eggs
120 ml (4 fl oz) water

1 Heat the oil in a frying pan over medium high heat and fry the sliced onion for 3–4 minutes until lightly browned.
2 Add the Onion Mix, turmeric, chili powder, salt and sugar and, stirring constantly, fry for another 2–3 minutes. Add the eggs and mix until they are covered with the spices.
3 Add the water, bring to a boil, lower the heat, cover and cook for about 10 minutes until the gravy thickens.

Fried Egg Curry
(Masala Andey)

Serves 4

3 medium onions	6 green
5 cloves garlic	cardamom pods
2.5 cm (1 in) ginger	2–3 green chilies
1 tbsp white vinegar	1½ tsp ground
8 tbsp mustard oil	turmeric
8 eggs	½ tsp chili powder
3 bay leaves	1 tsp salt
5 cm (2 in)	¼ tsp sugar
cinnamon stick	

1 Blend the onions, garlic, ginger and vinegar in a blender until you have a fine paste.

2 Heat the oil in a large frying pan over medium heat, fry the eggs one at a time and set aside.

3 To the remaining oil add the bay leaves, cinnamon and cardamom pods and let them sizzle for a few seconds.

4 Add the blended paste and the green chilies and fry for 6–8 minutes, stirring constantly. Add the turmeric, chili powder, salt and sugar and continue frying for another minute.

5 Carefully add the eggs and, stirring gently, cover them with some of the spices.

6 Cover and cook for 5 minutes. Serve hot with pilaf (see pages 120-124).

Omelet Curry

Serves 4
6 eggs
½ tsp salt
4 tbsp oil
1 large potato, cut into 2.5 cm (1 in) pieces
4 tbsp onion mix (see page 17)
1 tsp turmeric
½ tsp chili powder
¾ tsp salt
350 ml (12 fl oz) water

1 Whisk the eggs and the salt together.
2 Heat 1 tbsp of the oil in a large frying pan and make an omelet with half of the beaten eggs. Set aside and cut into four pieces. Similarly, make another omelet.
3 Heat the rest of the oil and fry the potato until lightly browned. Set aside. Add the onion mix and fry for 2–3 minutes. Add the turmeric, chili and salt and stir well with the onion mixture.
4 Add the water and bring to a boil. Put in the potatoes, cover, lower the heat and simmer for 10 minutes. Place the pieces of omelet in the pan, cover again and cook until the potatoes are tender, about another 10 minutes.

Yellow Rice with Hard-boiled Eggs
(Andey Ki Biriyani)

Serves 4–6

300–350 g (10–12 oz) basmati rice	600 ml (1 pt) boiling water
100 g (4 oz) butter or ghee (see page 16)	salt
1 small onion, chopped	½ tsp turmeric
2 cloves garlic, chopped	1 chicken stock cube, optional
1 green chili, chopped	10–15 cashew nuts
cardamom seeds from 2 pods	50 g (2 oz) ghee
2 bay leaves	25 g (1 oz) sultanas
3 cloves	4–6 hard-boiled eggs
	1 tsp lemon juice

1 Wash the rice thoroughly in 2 or 3 changes of water, then soak for 10–15 minutes.
2 Heat the butter or ghee in a pan, add the onion, garlic, green chili, cardamom seeds, bay leaves and cloves, and fry until the onion is golden.
3 Drain the rice, pour it into the pan, stir and fry for 10 minutes, until it turns translucent.
4 Pour on the boiling water, add ½ tsp salt, the turmeric and the stock cube, and simmer over low heat for 10 minutes. Turn off the heat and leave, covered, for 5 minutes until all the moisture has been absorbed and the grains of rice are separate and tender.
5 Fry the cashews for a couple of minutes in the ghee, adding the sultanas for the last few seconds.
6 Cut the eggs in half, sprinkle with lemon juice and rub with salt.
7 Spread the rice in a serving dish, sprinkle with salt to taste and arrange the eggs, cashew nuts and sultanas on top.

Whole Eggs Fried with Spice
(Andey Masala)

Serves 4
6 hard-boiled eggs
2 tbsp oil
2 tsp ground coriander
1 tsp chili powder
¼ tsp ground pepper
salt
2 tbsp lemon juice

1. Make several cuts into the eggs with the point of a sharp knife to allow the spices to enter.
2. Heat the oil, add the cilantro, chili powder, pepper and salt and fry for about 3 minutes.
3. Add the lemon juice and stir to make a paste.
4. Add the eggs to the saucepan and turn in the paste to coat. Continue cooking, turning occasionally, for 4–5 minutes.

Scrambled Eggs with Onion
(Piyaz Akuri)

Serves 2
1 small onion, finely chopped
1 tsp chili powder
2 curry leaves
2 eggs, beaten
salt
1–2 tbsp oil

1. Pound, grind, or blend in a blender the onion, chili powder and curry leaves, then mix with the beaten egg and ½ tsp salt.
2. Heat the oil in a pan, add the eggs and cook gently, stirring, until scrambled, for about 2 minutes.

Scrambled Eggs with Mushrooms and Shrimp
(Jhinga Kumban Ekuri)

Serves 2
2 tbsp oil
1 small onion, finely chopped
75 g (3 oz) mushrooms, peeled and sliced
75 g (3 oz) peeled shrimp
15 g (½ oz) fresh ginger, finely grated
1 green chili, finely chopped
75 g (3 oz) tomatoes, peeled and chopped
2 curry leaves
3 eggs, beaten
salt

1 Heat the oil in a pan, add the onion and fry until golden.
2 Add the mushrooms, shrimp, ginger, green chili, tomato and curry leaves and fry, stirring, for 5 minutes.
3 Add the eggs with ½ tsp salt and cook gently, stirring, for about 3 minutes, to scramble. (The eggs will continue to cook after you take them from the heat, so be careful not to over cook).

Spiced Scrambled Egg
(Ekuri)

Serves 2
2 eggs
1 small onion, finely chopped
1 green chili, finely chopped
2 curry leaves
15 g (½ oz) fresh ginger, finely grated
2 tbsp oil
salt

1 Beat the eggs well.
2 Stir the onion, chili, curry leaves and ginger together.
3 Heat the oil in a pan, add the onion mixture and fry for 3 minutes, stirring.
4 Add the eggs and cook gently, stirring, for about 2 minutes, until scrambled. (The eggs will continue cooking after you take them from the heat, so be careful not to over cook). Add salt to taste.

BREAD

Breads can be fried or grilled. An ordinary gas or electric oven can be used to broil Indian breads, but for best results a Tandoor should be used. This is a barrel-shaped clay oven that gives breads that special charcoal flavor. Try grilling breads and see how your friends react. Indians use these breads to eat their meals with their fingers. Tear a piece of bread and dip it into a plate of curry, or wrap a small piece of bread around a dry vegetable.

Whole Wheat Unleavened Bread
(Chappati)

275 g (10 oz) whole wheat flour
½ tsp salt
about 175 ml (6 fl oz) hot water
3 tbsp ghee (see page 16)

1 Sift the flour and salt together. Add enough water to form a soft dough.
2 Knead for about 10 minutes until no longer sticky. Cover and set aside for 1 hour.
3 Divide the dough into 12–14 balls. On a floured surface roll each ball into 15 cm (6 in) rounds.
4 Set the oven to broil and preheat until very hot.
5 Heat a frying pan over medium heat and place a chappati on it. Cook the chappati for 2 minutes until brown spots appear. Turn and cook the other side in the same way.
6 Take the chappati and place it under the broiler for a few seconds; it will puff up. Turn and cook the other side for a few seconds until it also puffs up.
7 Place the chappati in a dish and brush with a little ghee. Cover and keep warm while cooking the others.

Layered Bread
(Paratha)

350 g (12 oz) all-purpose flour
½ tsp salt
4 tbsp oil
about 175 ml (6 fl oz) hot water
3 tbsp ghee (see page 16)

1 Sift the flour and salt together. Rub in the oil.
2 Slowly add the water to form a soft dough. Knead for about 10 minutes until it is no longer sticky.
3 Divide the dough into 16 balls. Flatten a dough ball on a lightly floured surface with your hand and then roll into a 20 cm (8 in) circle.
4 Brush a little ghee on this and fold in half, brush on a little more ghee and fold into a small triangle. Roll out the triangle quite thinly on the floured surface.
5 Heat a frying pan over medium heat and place a rolled triangle on it. Heat each side for 1 minute until brown specks appear. Set aside. Cook each triangle in this manner.
6 Add the ghee and gently fry the parathas one at a time for 1–2 minutes, turning once, until golden brown. (While cooking the parathas, keep the fried ones warm by wrapping them in foil).

Corn Meal Bread
(Makki Ki Roti)

300 g (11 oz) coarse corn meal
pinch of salt
about 120 ml (4 fl oz) hot water
ghee (see page 16)

1 Sift the polenta and salt together.
2 Add enough water to make a stiff dough. Knead with your palms for about 10 minutes until soft and smooth.
3 Divide the dough into 8–10 balls.
4 Take one of the balls and place it on a lightly floured surface and, with the palm of your hand, press the ball gently to about 13 cm (5 in) diameter and less than 5 mm (¼ in) thick. (If the dough tends to stick to your hand place a little flour on top of the dough).
5 Gently lift the roti and place on a hot tava or frying pan and cook until golden. Turn and cook the other side in the same way.
6 Pierce the roti a few times with a fork, and brush with the ghee. Make all the rotis in the same way. Serve with Spicy Mustard Leaves (see page 47).

Deep-fried White Bread
(Lucchi)

350 g (12 oz) all-purpose flour
½ tsp salt
2 tbsp oil
about 175 ml (6 fl oz) hot water
oil for deep frying

1 Sift the flour and salt together. Rub in the oil.
2 Slowly add enough water to form a stiff dough. Knead for about 10 minutes until you have a soft, pliable dough.
3 Divide the dough into about 40 small balls and flatten each ball.
4 Roll out a few balls on a slightly oily surface into rounds of 10 cm (4 in) across (do not roll out all the balls at the same time as they tend to stick).
5 Heat the oil in a karai over high heat. Put in a lucchi and press the middle with a slotted spoon as this causes the lucchi to puff up. Turn and cook the other side for a few seconds. Drain and serve hot.

Leavened Bread
(Naan)

1 tsp dried yeast
1 tsp sugar
75 ml (3 fl oz) lukewarm water
275 g (10 oz) all-purpose flour
½ tsp salt
¾ tsp baking powder
1 tbsp oil
about 3 tbsp plain yogurt

1 Stir the yeast and sugar into the water and set aside for 15–20 minutes until the liquid is frothy.
2 Sift together the flour, salt and baking powder. Make a well in the middle, add the yeast liquid, oil and yogurt and knead for about 10 minutes until soft and no longer sticky.
3 Place the dough in an oiled plastic bag and set aside in a warm place for 2–3 hours until it doubles in size.
4 Preheat the oven to 200°C/400°F/Gas Mark 6. Knead the dough again for 1–2 minutes and divide into 12 balls. Roll into 18 cm (7 in) rounds.
5 Place as many as possible on a baking sheet and put in the oven for around 4–5 minutes each side, until brown spots appear. Place them under a hot broiler for a few seconds until slightly browned.
6 Wrap the cooked ones in foil while cooking the others.

Yogurt Bread
(Batora)

225 g (8 oz) all-purpose flour
1½ tsp baking powder
½ tsp salt
1 tsp sugar
1 egg, beaten
about 3 tbsp yogurt
oil for deep frying

1 Sift the flour, baking powder and salt together. Mix in the sugar.
2 Add the beaten egg and enough yogurt to form a stiff dough. Knead for 10–15 minutes until you have a soft, smooth dough. Cover with a cloth and let it rest for 3–4 hours.
3 Knead again on a floured surface for 5 minutes. Divide into 12–14 balls.
4 Roll out on a floured surface into 12.5 cm (5 in) rounds.
5 Heat the oil in a karai over high heat. Fry the batoras, pressing in the middle with a slotted spoon so that they puff up. Turn and cook the other side for a few seconds until lightly browned. Drain. Serve hot with Spiced Chickpeas or Soured Chickpeas (see pages 38-39).

Stuffed Deep-fried Bread
(Mater Kachori)

Filling
1 tbsp ghee (see page 16)
pinch of asafetida
5 mm (¾ in) fresh ginger, grated
225 g (8 oz) peas, boiled and mashed
¼ tsp chili powder
¼ tsp salt
½ tsp garam masala (see page 17)

Dough
225 g (8 oz) all-purpose flour
½ tsp salt
1½ tsp ghee
approx 120 ml (4 fl oz) hot water
oil for deep frying

1 To make the filling, heat the ghee in a karai over medium heat, add the asafetida and ginger and fry for a few seconds.
2 Add the mashed peas, chili powder and salt and, stirring constantly, fry for about 5 minutes until the mixture leaves the sides and forms a ball. Mix in the garam masala and set aside to cool.
3 To make the dough, sift the flour and salt together. Rub in the ghee. Add enough water to make a stiff dough. Knead for about 10 minutes to form a soft pliable dough. Divide into 20 balls.
4 Insert your thumb into the middle of each ball to form a cup. Fill with 1 tsp of the filling. Seal the top and reshape into a ball.
5 Flatten and roll into 10 cm (4 in) rounds on a slightly oiled surface (take care that no holes appear when rolling).
6 Heat the oil in a karai until very hot. Gently put in a kachori and press the middle so that it puffs up. Turn and fry the other side until lightly golden. Drain on paper towels and serve hot with Potato Masala Curry (see page 58).

Deep-fried Brown Bread
(Poori)

225 g (8 oz) whole wheat flour
½ tsp salt
2 tbsp oil
about 90 ml (3 fl oz) hot water
oil for deep frying

1 Sift together the flour and salt. Rub in the oil. Add enough water to make a stiff dough.
2 Put the dough on a floured surface and knead for about 10 minutes until soft and smooth.
3 Divide the mixture into 20 balls.
4 Taking one ball at a time, flatten them on a slightly oiled surface and roll into rounds of 10 cm (4 in) across. (Do not stack the rolled pooris on top of one another as they might stick together).
5 Heat the oil in a karai until very hot and add a poori, pressing the middle with a slotted spoon so that it puffs up. Quickly turn and cook the other side for a few seconds. Drain and serve hot.

Stuffed Potato Bread
(Aloo Paratha)

Filling
450 g (1 lb) potatoes, boiled and mashed
1 small onion, finely chopped
1–2 green chilies, finely chopped
1 tbsp chopped cilantro leaves
¾ tsp salt
¾ tsp roast ground cumin (see page 18)

Dough
350 g (12 oz) all-purpose flour
½ tsp salt
4 tbsp oil
about 175 ml (6 fl oz) hot water
ghee (see page 16) for frying

1 To make the filling, mix all the ingredients together and set aside.

2 To make the dough, sift the flour and salt together. Rub in the oil. Add enough water to form a stiff dough. Knead for about 10 minutes until you have a smooth dough. Divide into 20 balls.

3 Roll out two balls into 10 cm (4 in) rounds. Place about 1½–2 tbsp of the filling on one of the rounds and spread it evenly. Place the other round over the filling, sealing the edges with a little water.

4 Roll out gently into 18 cm (7 in) rounds, making sure that no filling comes out. Roll out all the parathas in a similar manner.

5 Heat a frying pan over medium heat. Place a paratha in the frying pan and cook for about 1 minute until brown spots appear. Turn and cook the other side.

6 Add 2 tsp of ghee and cook for 2–3 minutes until golden brown. Turn and cook the other side, adding more ghee if required. Make all the parathas in the same way. Serve warm.

RICE

The "King of Rice" is the basmati variety that comes from Dehradun – one of the hill stations founded by the British as a summer retreat. This rice has a unique flavor when cooked and is by far the best quality. Other types of rice are Pakistani basmati rice, patna rice and joha rice. American long-grain rice is also adequate for the preparation of Indian meals.

Plain Rice
(Sada Chawal)

Serves 4
350 g (12 oz) basmati rice
900 ml (2 pt) cold water

1 Rinse the rice three or four times in cold water. Drain.
2 Place the drained rice in a large saucepan and pour in the measured amount of water. Bring it to a boil rapidly over high heat. Stir.
3 Lower the heat to very low, cover and cook for about 20 minutes until all the water has evaporated.
4 Fluff the rice with a fork and serve hot.

Rice with Yogurt
(Dahi Chawal)

Serves 4
225 g (8 oz) yogurt
275–350 g (10–12 oz) cooked basmati rice
2 tbsp oil
2 tsp polished split black lentils (urid dal)
1 tsp mustard seeds
4–6 curry leaves
2 red or green chilies, chopped
salt

1 Mix the yogurt into the rice, without mashing the grains.
2 Heat the oil in a pan, add the dal and fry until light brown.
3 Add the mustard seeds, curry leaves and chili and fry until all the seeds have popped.
4 Stir the contents of the saucepan into the rice, mixing carefully, and add salt to taste.

Fried Rice
(Ghee Bhat)

Serves 4

3 tbsp ghee (see page 16)
2 bay leaves
5 cm (2 in) cinnamon stick
4 green cardamom pods
3 large onions, finely sliced
3 green chilies, cut lengthways
350 g (12 oz) basmati rice, cooked and cooled
1 tsp salt
½ tsp sugar
2 tbsp raisins (optional)

1 Heat the ghee in a large frying pan over medium high heat. Add the bay leaves, cinnamon and cardamom and let them sizzle for a few seconds.

2 Add the onions and chilies and fry until the onions are golden brown.

3 Add the rice, salt, sugar and raisins and continue frying until the rice is thoroughly heated through.

Tomato Rice
(Tamatar Chawal)

Serves 4
2 tbsp oil
½ tsp mustard seeds
2 tbsp split gram, soaked in water
    for 20 minutes, then drained
6 curry leaves
1 red chili, cut into pieces
1 onion, chopped
15 g (½ oz) fresh ginger, finely grated
2 cloves garlic, sliced
1 green chili, chopped
350 g (12 oz) tomatoes, peeled and chopped
1 tsp sugar
275–350 g (10–12 oz) cooked basmati rice
1 tsp ghee (see page 16)
salt

1 Heat the oil in a pan, add the mustard seeds, split gram, curry leaves and red chili and fry until all the mustard seeds have popped and the gram is golden brown.
2 Add the onion, ginger, garlic and green chili and fry for 3–5 minutes, stirring.
3 Add the tomato and sugar and cook, mashing the tomato under the back of a wooden spoon to make a thick paste.
4 Stir in the rice and ghee and heat through, stirring, for about 5 minutes until hot. Add extra salt to taste.

Lemon Rice
(Nimbowala Chawal)

Serves 4
275–350 g (10–12 oz) cooked basmati rice
2 tbsp lemon juice
¼ tsp asafetida
½ tsp turmeric
salt
2 tbsp oil
½ tsp mustard seeds
1 tsp polished split black lentils (urid dal)
6 curry leaves
2 tbsp split gram, soaked in water
    for 20 minutes, then drained
15 g (½ oz) fresh ginger, finely grated
1 green chili, chopped

1 Mix the rice with the lemon juice, asafetida, turmeric and salt to taste.
2 Heat the oil in a pan, add the mustard seeds, dal, curry leaves and split gram and fry until all the mustard seeds have popped.
3 Add the ginger, green chili and rice and heat through, stirring, for about 5 minutes, until hot.
4 Add extra salt to taste.

Spiced Rice
(Masale Bhat)

Serves 4

275 g (10 oz) basmati rice
3 tsp cilantro seeds
2 tsp cumin seeds
1 cm (½ in) cinnamon stick
Seeds from 3 green cardamom pods, shelled
2 cloves
3 tbsp oil
¾ tsp mustard seeds
good pinch of asafetida
½ tsp ground turmeric
1 tsp chili powder
1 small cauliflower, chopped into small pieces
750 ml (1½ pt) water
1½ tsp salt
3 tbsp chopped cilantro leaves, optional
3 tbsp grated coconut, optimal
ghee (see page 16)

1 Wash the rice in several changes of water and soak for 1 hour in plenty of water. Drain the rice and leave in a sieve for about 20 minutes.

2 While the rice is soaking, dry roast the cilantro, cumin, cinnamon, cardamom and cloves over a medium heat, until they are a few shades darker and emit a rich aroma.

3 Grind the spices into a fine powder and put aside.

4 In a large saucepan, heat the oil, add the mustard seeds and let them sizzle for 5–6 seconds. Add the asafetida, turmeric, chili powder and cauliflower and, taking care not to burn the spices, stirfry for 1–2 minutes.

5 Add the rice and sauté for a few minutes, making sure that the rice does not brown.

6 Add the water, bring to a boil, give it a good stir, lower the heat to very low, cover and cook for 8 minutes. Remove the cover, add the powdered spices and salt, mix, cover again and cook for a further 10 minutes until all the water is absorbed.

7 Fluff gently with a fork. Garnish with the cilantro leaves and coconut, if you wish. Serve hot with ghee.

Rice with Legumes
(Khichuri)

Serves 4

75 g (3 oz) moong dal
75 g (3 oz) red lentils, washed
6 tbsp oil
2 bay leaves
5 cm (2 in) cinnamon stick
4 green cardamom pods
3 cloves garlic, crushed
2.5 cm (1 in) fresh ginger, grated
1 large onion, finely sliced
1 tsp ground turmeric
½ tsp chili powder
1 tsp salt
⅓ tsp sugar
1 tomato, chopped
75 g (3 oz) basmati rice, washed and drained
1.25 l (2½ pt) water
3–4 green chilies, halved lengthways

1. In a small saucepan dry roast the moong dal over medium heat, until it turns light brown. Remove from the heat, wash thoroughly, and mix with the red lentils. Put in a sieve to drain.
2. Heat the oil in a large saucepan over medium heat. Add the bay leaves, cinnamon stick and cardamom pods and let them sizzle for a few seconds.
3. Add the garlic, ginger and onion and fry until the onion is golden brown.
4. Add the turmeric, chili powder, salt, sugar and tomato and mix thoroughly. Add the rice and the legumes and continue to fry for 5–7 minutes.
5. Add the water, and when it starts to boil, lower the heat and simmer for about 35–40 minutes.
6. Just before removing from the heat, add the chilies. Serve with ghee (see page 16) and Pakoras (see page 135).

Simple Rice with Legumes

Serves 3–4

225 g (8 oz) basmati rice, washed and drained
50 g (2 oz) moong dal, washed and drained
750 ml (1½ pt) water
1½ tbsp ghee (see page 16)

1 Mix the rice and dal and soak in plenty of water for 1 hour. Drain.
2 Add the rice and dal mixture to the measured water in a large saucepan and bring to a boil over high heat. Turn the heat down to very low, cover and cook for about 20 minutes until all the water has been absorbed. Remove from the heat.
3 In a small pan, heat the ghee until very hot and pour it over the cooked rice and dal. Mix. Serve hot with Spinach with Legumes and Vegetables (see page 48), yogurt and poppadoms.

Potato Pilaf
(Aloo Pillau)

Serves 4–6

75 g (3 oz) creamed coconut
600 ml (1 pt) hot water
handful cilantro leaves
1 tbsp grated coconut
2 green chilies
2 tbsp lemon juice
½ tsp sugar
1½ tsp salt
½ tsp garam masala (see page 17)
¼ tsp ground turmeric
10–12 small new potatoes, washed and peeled
3 tbsp oil
2 cloves
1 medium onion, finely sliced
1 clove garlic, crushed
275 g (10 oz) basmati rice, washed and drained

1 Make the coconut milk by blending together the creamed coconut and hot water. Put aside.
2 Chop the cilantro leaves and throw away the lower stalks and roots. Wash them thoroughly.
3 Blend together the cilantro leaves, grated coconut, chilies, lemon juice, sugar, ½ tsp salt, garam masala and turmeric until you have a fine paste.
4 Parboil the potatoes. Drain and cool.
5 Take a potato and make two cuts like a cross coming about three-quarters of the way down the length. Take care not to cut all the way through. Cut all the potatoes in this way.
6 Fill each potato with a little of the cilantro paste. If you have any paste left, rub it onto the potatoes.
7 Heat the oil over medium high heat in a large saucepan. Add the cloves and, after 3–4 seconds, add the onion and garlic and fry until the onion is lightly golden.
8 Add the rice and sauté for 2–3 minutes, stirring constantly.
9 Add the coconut milk and 1 tsp salt and bring to a boil. Add the potatoes, and when it comes to a boil again, lower the heat to very low, cover and cook for about 20 minutes until all the water has been absorbed.
10 Fluff the rice with a fork before serving.

Pea Pilaf
(Mater Pillau)

Serves 4–6

3 tbsp oil
½ tsp whole cumin seeds
1 medium onion, finely chopped
100 g (4 oz) peas
350 g (12 oz) basmati rice, washed and drained
1 tsp salt
900 ml (2 pt) water

1 Heat the oil in a large saucepan over medium heat, add the cumin seeds and let them sizzle for a few seconds.
2 Add the onion and fry until soft. Add the peas, rice and salt and stirfry for about 5 minutes. Add the water and bring to a boil.
3 Cover tightly, lower the heat to very low and cook for about 20 minutes until all the water has been absorbed. Fluff the pilaf with a fork and serve hot.

Vegetable Pilaf
(Sabzi Ka Pillau)

Serves 4–6

275 g (10 oz) basmati rice
5 tbsp ghee (see page 16)
2 tbsp unsalted cashew nuts
1 medium onion, finely chopped
1 cm (½ in) ginger, cut into very thin strips
225 (8 oz) green beans, cut into
    4 cm (1½ in) lengths
2 small carrots, peeled and diced
75 g (3 oz) peas
1 small red pepper, seeded and thinly sliced
900 ml (2 pt) water
1½ tsp salt
1 tbsp cilantro leaves

1   Wash the rice in several changes of water and leave in a sieve to drain thoroughly.
2   Heat the ghee in a large saucepan and fry the cashews until golden. Drain and put aside.
3   In the remaining ghee, add the onion and ginger and fry until the onion is soft and transparent.
4   Add the rice and stirfry for 1–2 minutes. Add all the vegetables and mix with the onion and rice.
5   Add the water and salt and bring to a boil. Give it a good stir, lower the heat to very low, cover and cook for about 20 minutes until the rice and vegetables are tender and all the water is absorbed.
6   Garnish with the fried cashews and cilantro leaves.

Pilaf with Coconut and Milk
(Narial Aur Dudh Pillau)

Serves 4

350 g (12 oz) basmati rice, rinsed and drained
2 tbsp dried coconut
2–3 green chilies
1 tsp salt
½ tsp sugar
2 tbsp raisins
1 tbsp pistachio nuts, skinned and
    cut into thin strips
2 bay leaves
5 cm (2 in) cinnamon stick
4 green cardamom pods
3 tbsp ghee (see page 16)
600 ml (1 pt) milk
300 ml (½ pt) water

1   Mix the rice with the coconut, chilies, salt, sugar, raisins, pistachios, bay leaves, cinnamon and cardamom pods.
2   Heat the ghee in a large saucepan over medium heat. Add the rice mixture and sauté for 5 minutes, stirring constantly.
3   Add the milk and water, increase the heat to high and bring to a boil. Stir.
4   Lower the heat to very low, cover and cook for about 20 minutes until all the liquid has evaporated. Fluff the pilaf with a fork and serve hot.

Mushroom Pilaf
(Khumbi Pillau)

Serves 4–6

2 tbsp oil
2 bay leaves
5 cm (2 in) cinnamon stick
4 green cardamom pods
1 large onion, finely chopped
175 g (6 oz) mushrooms, sliced
350 g (12 oz) basmati rice, washed and drained
1 tsp salt
900 ml (2 pt) water

1 Heat the oil in a large saucepan over medium high heat. Add the bay leaves, cinnamon and cardamom pods and let them sizzle for a few seconds.

2 Add the onion and fry until soft. Add the mushrooms and fry for about 5 minutes until all the moisture has been absorbed.

3 Add the rice and salt and stirfry for 2–3 minutes. Add the water and bring to a boil.

4 Cover tightly, lower the heat to very low and cook for about 20 minutes until all the water has been absorbed. Fluff the pilaf with a fork and serve hot.

SNACKS AND SALADS

These snack recipes are extremely versatile. They are ideal for picnics as they can be eaten cold, served with a salad or chutney. They can form part of a meal as a side dish with a main course, or alternatively, as an hors d'oeuvre.

Spicy Pounded Rice
(Batata Poha)

Serves 4

100 g (4 oz) cooked, pounded rice
2 tbsp oil
½ tsp mustard seeds
1–2 dried red chilies, broken in half
1–2 green chilies, chopped
5–6 curry leaves
1 small onion, finely chopped
2 medium potatoes, boiled and diced
    into 1 cm (½ in) cubes
¼ tsp ground turmeric
1 tsp salt
½ tsp chili powder
2 tsp lime juice
2 tbsp cilantro leaves, chopped

1 Wash the pounded rice and leave to drain in a sieve for about 15 minutes.
2 Heat the oil over medium high heat and add the mustard seeds; as soon as they start to splutter add the red chilies, green chilies and curry leaves and let them sizzle for 7–8 seconds.
3 Add the onion and stirfry until golden.
4 Add the potatoes, turmeric, salt and chili powder and mix with the onions.
5 Add the drained pounded rice and mix with the other ingredients; stirfry for 2–3 minutes.
6 Lower the heat, cover and cook for about 8–10 minutes, stirring occasionally (add a little extra oil if necessary).
7 Sprinkle on the lime juice and cilantro leaves. Mix well and serve immediately. This is eaten for breakfast or as a light snack.

Savory Puffed Rice
(Bhel Poori)

Serves 4–6

700 g (1½ lb) puffed rice
1 medium potato, boiled and diced
    into 5 mm (¼ in) cubes
1 small onion, finely chopped
2 tbsp cilantro leaves, chopped
½ tsp salt

Tamarind chutney	Green chutney
about 120 ml (4 fl oz) thick tamarind juice	4 sprigs of cilantro, washed
½ tsp salt	2 green chilies
½ tsp chili powder	½ tsp salt
½ tsp sugar	2–3 tbsp lemon juice
	a little water

1 Mix together the puffed rice, potato, onion, cilantro leaves and salt and put aside.
2 Make the tamarind chutney by mixing together the tamarind juice, salt, chili powder and sugar; put aside.
3 Make the green chutney by first chopping the cilantro leaves and throwing away the lower stalks and roots.
4 Blend together the cilantro leaves, green chilies, salt and lemon juice until smooth. Add a little water if necessary. This sauce should not be too thick.
5 When you are ready to serve the bhel poori, add the chutneys to the puffed rice mixture (the amount can vary according to individual taste). Serve immediately as a snack.

Rice with Gram Flour Dumplings
(Gatte Ki Khichiri)

Serves 4

75 g (3 oz) gram flour	**Rice**
¼ tsp chili powder	275 g (10 oz)
½ tsp ground	basmati rice
coriander	2 tbsp ghee
pinch of turmeric	1 tsp cumin seeds
½ tsp salt	½ tsp chili powder
2 tbsp ghee	900 ml (2 pt)
(see page 16)	boiling water
about 4 tbsp hot water	

1 Sift the gram flour into a large bowl.

2 Mix in the chili powder, cilantro, turmeric and half of the salt. Rub in the ghee.

3 Add enough water to make a firm dough and knead for 2–3 minutes.

4 Divide into 4 parts. Roll each ball into round strips 15 cm (6 in) long.

5 Bring some water to the boil and place these strips carefully in the water. Boil for 5 minutes. Drain and cool, then cut into 1 cm (½ in) pieces.

6 Wash the basmati rice in several changes of water. Leave the rice to soak for 20 minutes in plenty of water then drain.

7 In a large saucepan, heat the ghee over medium high heat. Add the cumin seeds and let them sizzle for 3–4 seconds.

8 Add the rice, chili powder and remaining salt, and sauté for 2–3 minutes.

9 Add the gram flour pieces carefully and gently mix with the rice. Fry for 1 minute.

10 Add the water and, when it starts to boil rapidly, lower the heat to very low, cover and cook for about 20 minutes until the rice is tender.

11 Fluff with a fork and serve hot.

Curry with Gram Flour Dumplings
(Gatte Ki Saag)

Serves 4

Dough	Curry
75 g (3 oz) gram flour	2 tbsp ghee (see page 16)
¼ tsp chili powder	½ tsp cumin seeds
½ tsp ground coriander	¼ tsp mustard seeds
good pinch of turmeric	pinch of asafetida
¾ tsp salt	120 ml (4 fl oz) yogurt, beaten well
2 tbsp ghee (see page 16)	½ tsp chili powder
about 4 tbsp water	3 tsp ground coriander
	½ tsp ground turmeric
	1 tsp salt
	pinch of asafetida

1 To make the dough, place the gram flour, chili powder, cilantro, turmeric and salt in a bowl. Rub in the ghee.
2 Add enough water to make a firm dough. Knead for 2–3 minutes.
3 Divide into 4 parts. Roll each ball between your palms into round strips 15 cm (6 in) long.
4 Bring some water to a boil, and place the strips into the water carefully. Boil for 5 minutes. Drain and cool. Cut into 1 cm (1½ in) pieces.
5 To make the curry, heat the ghee in a saucepan over medium heat. Add the cumin seeds, mustard and asafetida and let them splutter for 5–6 seconds.
6 Remove from the heat and add the yogurt and the rest of the spices.
7 Stirring constantly, return the saucepan to the heat and cook for about 3–4 minutes (if you do not stir constantly the yogurt might separate).
8 Add the gram flour pieces, mix gently with the gravy and cook for 5 more minutes.

Fried Lentil Cakes
(Vada)

Serves 4

225 g (8 oz) channa dal, washed	pinch of asafetida
1–2 green chilies, chopped	½ tsp chili powder (optional)
1 small onion, finely chopped	½ tsp salt
	oil for deep frying

1 Soak the dal in plenty of cold water for 4–5 hours. Drain.
2 Grind the dal coarsely in a food processor or blender. (If using a blender, add a little water only if necessary).
3 Add the green chilies, onion, asafetida, chili powder and salt to the ground dal and mix well.
4 Heat the oil over medium high heat.
5 Take 1 tbsp of the mixture in the palm of your hand, flatten it slightly and deep fry for 1–2 minutes until golden brown. Make all the lentil cakes in this way. Serve hot.

Spicy Lamb Wrapped with Potatoes
(Chop)

Serves 4

Filling

2 tbsp oil

1 large onion,
  finely sliced

2 cloves garlic,
  crushed

1 cm (½ in)
  ginger, grated

¾ tsp ground turmeric

½ tsp chili powder

1 tsp salt

good pinch of sugar

1 tbsp raisins (optional)

2 tsp vinegar

450 g (1 lb) ground
  lamb

1 tsp ground garam
  masala
  (see page 17)

1 egg (slightly beaten)

breadcrumbs

oil for shallow frying

Chop

750 g (1¾ lb) potatoes,
  peeled and boiled

1 tsp ground
  roast cumin

½ tsp ground, roast,
  dried red chilies
  (optional)

1 tsp salt

1 To make the filling, heat the oil in a large frying pan over medium high heat. Add the onion, garlic and ginger and fry for 4–5 minutes, stirring constantly, until the onion turns pale gold.

2 Add the turmeric, chili powder, salt, sugar, raisins and vinegar, mix thoroughly with the onion and fry for 1 minute. Add the lamb and mix with the spices.

3 Cover, lower the heat, and, stirring occasionally, cook for about 20 minutes. Remove the cover, turn the heat up and, stirring constantly, cook until all the liquid has evaporated and the lamb is dry.

4 Mix in the garam masala, remove from the heat and set aside to cool.

5 To make the chop, mash the potatoes with the cumin, chili and salt. Divide into 20–22 balls.

6 Take a ball and make a depression in the middle with your thumb, to form a cup shape. Fill the center with the meat and re-form the potato ball, making sure no cracks appear. Make all the chop in this manner. (The chop can be round and flat or long in shape).

7 Place the chop in the beaten egg, one at a time, and roll in the breadcrumbs.

8 Heat the oil over very high heat in a large frying pan and fry the chop until golden brown, turning once (about 1 minute).

Fried Potatoes
(Aloo Bhaja)

Serves 2

3–4 medium potatoes, peeled
½ tsp salt
oil for shallow frying

1 Slice the potatoes thinly and rub in the salt.
2 Heat the oil over high heat and fry the potatoes until golden.

Fried Fish
(Mach Bhaja)

Serves 2

1 tsp salt
½ tsp ground turmeric
450 g (1 lb) medium-sized herring, cleaned and washed
oil for shallow frying

1 Rub the salt and turmeric into the fish and set aside for 15–20 minutes.
2 Heat the oil over medium high heat and fry the fish for about 3–4 minutes on each side.

Fried Potato Cakes
(Aloo Tikka)

Serves 4

450 g (1 lb) potatoes, boiled and mashed
1–2 green chilies, chopped
½ tsp salt
1 tbsp cilantro leaves, chopped
2 tbsp onions, chopped
oil for frying

1 Mix the mashed potatoes with the chilies, salt, cilantro leaves and onions.
2 Form into small balls and flatten.
3 Heat the oil until hot and fry the potato cakes for a few minutes on each side until golden. Serve with a chutney.

Fried Eggplant
(Baigun Bhaja)

Serves 2

1 large eggplant
½ tsp salt
pinch of ground turmeric
pinch of sugar
oil for shallow frying

1 Slice the eggplant into 1 cm (½ in) thick rounds. Rub with the salt, turmeric and sugar and leave in a sieve for 30 minutes for the excess water to drain out.

2 Heat the oil over medium high heat and fry the eggplant until brown, turning once.

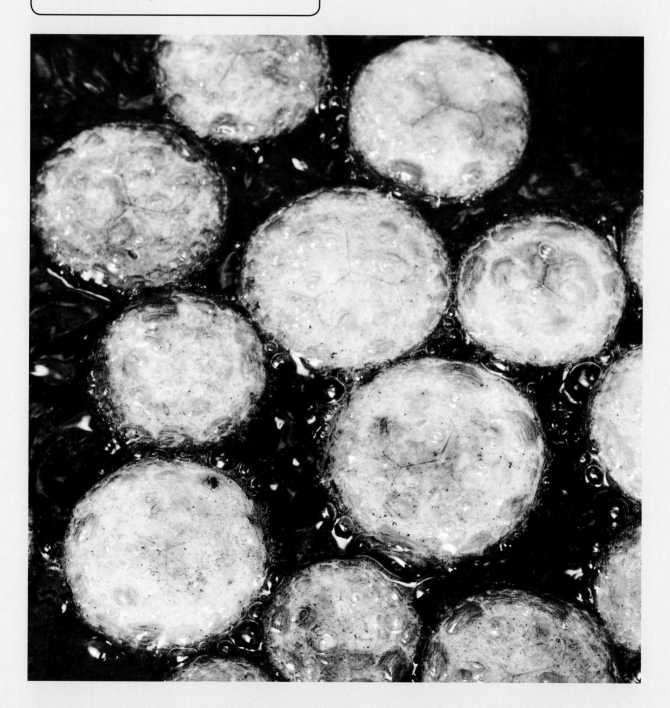

Vegetable Cutlet
(Sabze Cutlet)

Serves 4
100 g (4 oz) beets, diced
100 g (4 oz) carrots, diced
225 g (8 oz) potatoes, diced
100 g (4 oz) cabbage, grated
½ tsp chili powder
½ tsp ground roast cumin (see page 18)
½ tsp ground black pepper
¾ tsp salt
a big pinch of sugar
1 tbsp raisins (optional)
50 g (2 oz) flour
120 ml (4 fl oz) milk
breadcrumbs
oil for deep frying

1 Boil the beets, carrots, potatoes and cabbage together until tender. Drain.
2 Mash the boiled vegetables with the chili powder, roast cumin, black pepper, salt, sugar and raisins. Divide into 12 balls and flatten. Chill for 1 hour.
3 Make a batter with the flour and milk and dip each cutlet in it. Then roll in breadcrumbs until well coated.
4 Heat the oil in a large frying pan and fry the cutlets for 2–3 minutes, turning once, until crisp and golden. Serve with Green Cilantro Chutney (see page 152).

Plantain Balls
(Kela Kofta)

Serves 2
1 plantain, cut in half
1 green chili, chopped
½ tbsp chopped cilantro leaves
½ tsp salt
1 tbsp onion, chopped
1 tsp all-purpose flour
oil for deep frying

1 Boil the plantain until soft. Peel and cool.
2 Mash the plantain with the chili, cilantro leaves, salt, onion and flour. Divide the mixture into 8 small balls and flatten.
3 Heat the oil and fry the koftas, turning once, until crisp and golden.

Pastry with Potato Stuffing
(Bhakhar Vadi)

Serves 4

700 g (1½ lb) potatoes, washed and peeled
2 green chilies
1 cm (½ in) ginger
3 tbsp oil
½ tsp mustard seeds
pinch of asafetida
2 dried red chilies
¼ tsp chili powder
pinch of ground turmeric
2 tsp salt
1½ tsp dried mango powder (amchur)
½ tsp sugar
225 g (8 oz) wholemeal flour
100 g (4 oz) all-purpose flour
about 5 tbsp warm water
oil for deep frying

1 Finely grate the potatoes and soak in water for about 30 minutes. Drain and dry thoroughly.

2 Grind the green chilies and ginger into a paste.

3 Heat 2 tbsp of the oil over medium high heat. Add the mustard, asafetida and red chilies and let them sizzle for 8–10 seconds.

4 Add the potatoes, chili powder, turmeric, 1 tsp salt and the chili and ginger paste and stirfry for 5–7 minutes.

5 Lower the heat slightly, cover and, stirring occasionally, cook for about 25–30 minutes until the potatoes are tender. Add the mango powder and sugar, and mix. Remove from the heat, cool and divide into 4 parts.

6 Sift together the wholemeal flour, all-purpose flour and 1 tsp salt. Rub in 1 tbsp of oil.

7 Add enough water to make a stiff dough. Knead for 7–10 minutes to make the dough soft and pliable. Divide into 4.

8 Take a portion and roll into a 20 cm (8 in) round on a lightly floured surface. Spread a portion of the potato mixture evenly on the rolled dough. Starting at the side closest to you, carefully roll it up tightly like a Swiss roll. Cut into slices 1 cm (½ in) thick. Gently flatten each slice between the palms of your hands.

9 Heat the oil for deep frying and carefully fry pastries for 3–4 minutes until they are golden; turn once. These can be eaten as a snack or as an accompaniment to a main meal.

Rice and Lentil Pancakes with Potato Stuffing
(Masala Dosa)

Serves 4

200 g (7 oz) rice, washed
65 g (2½ oz) split black lentils (urid dal), washed
1 tsp salt
about 175 ml (6 fl oz) water
a little oil for frying

Filling

4 tbsp oil
½ tsp mustard seeds
1 tbsp channa dal
⅓ tsp asafetida
2 tbsp cashew nuts, chopped (optional)
8–10 curry leaves
2 cm (¾ in) ginger, grated
3–4 green chilies, chopped
1 large onion, finely sliced
450 g (1 lb) potatoes, peeled and diced into
   5 mm (¼ in) cubes and then boiled
½ tsp ground turmeric
1 tsp salt
120 ml (4 fl oz) water

1 Soak the rice and urid dal separately in plenty of water and set aside for 6–8 hours. Drain.

2 In a blender or food processor, blend the rice and dal separately to a fine paste. During the blending add a little water, if required.

3 Mix the two pastes together, add the salt and beat for 1–2 minutes.

4 Cover and set aside in a warm place overnight to let it ferment.

5 The next morning, give the mixture a good stir and add enough water to make a thin pouring consistency.

6 To make the filling, heat 4 tbsp oil in a saucepan over medium high heat, add the mustard seeds, channa dal, asafetida, cashews, curry leaves, ginger and green chilies and let them sizzle for 6–8 seconds.

7 Add the onion and fry until transparent.

8 Add the potatoes, turmeric and salt and mix with the other spices. Add the water, bring to a boil, cover and simmer over medium heat for about 10 minutes until well mixed and all the water has evaporated. Put aside.

9 To make the pancakes, heat a non-stick frying pan over medium heat and brush with a little oil. Pour in a ladleful of the mixture and spread it like a pancake. Put a little more oil around the edges and a little on top. Cook for a couple of minutes until lightly golden. Turn the dosa and cook for another couple of minutes.

10 Put on a plate, place a heaped tbsp of the hot filling on one end of the dosa, fold in half and serve hot with Coconut Chutney (see page 150) and Lentils with Vegetables II (see page 24). (It can also be folded to make a triangle).

Vegetable Fritters
(Pakoras)

Serves 4

Batter
4 tbsp gram flour
2 tsp oil
1 tsp baking powder
½ tsp salt
85 ml (3 fl oz) water

Any of the following vegetables can be used:
eggplants, cut into very thin rounds
onions, cut into 2 mm (⅛ in) rings
potatoes, cut into very thin rounds
cauliflower, cut into 2 cm (¾ in) florets
chili, left whole
pumpkin, cut into thin slices
green pepper, cut into thin strips
oil for deep frying

1 Mix all the batter ingredients together and beat until smooth.
2 Wash the pieces of vegetable and pat dry.
3 Heat the oil in a karai until it is very hot.
4 Dip a piece of the vegetable in the batter and put into the hot oil. Place as many pieces as you can in the oil. Fry until crisp and golden.
5 Drain and serve with either Green Cilantro or Mint Chutney (see pages 152 and 153).

Savory Semolina
(Uppuma)

Serves 4

175 g (6 oz) coarse semolina
2 tbsp unsalted peanuts, chopped
3 tbsp oil
¼ tsp mustard seeds
2 tsp split black lentils (urid dal)
1 tsp channa dal
1 medium onion, finely chopped
10–12 curry leaves
1 small carrot, cut into thin strips
 about 5 cm (2 in) long
2 tbsp peas
4–5 green beans, cut into thin strips
 about 5 cm (2 in) long
1 tsp salt
about 750 ml (1½ pt) water
juice of ½ a lemon

1 Dry roast the semolina until lightly golden.
 Set aside.
2 Dry roast the peanuts until golden and put aside.
3 Heat the oil over medium heat, add the mustard
 seeds, urid and channa dals and when they
 stop spluttering, add the onion and 8 of the curry
 leaves. Fry until the onion is golden.
4 Add the vegetables and stirfry for 2–3 minutes.
5 Add the semolina and mix with the other
 ingredients and continue to fry for 1–2 more
 minutes.
6 Add the salt and water and, stirring constantly,
 cook until all the water evaporates and the mixture
 is absolutely dry.
7 Squeeze over the lemon juice and mix in the
 remaining curry leaves.
8 Garnish with the roast peanuts. Serve hot with
 Coconut Chutney (see page 150) as a light meal.

Savory Potato Snack
(Aloo Kabli)

Serves 2

350 g (12 oz) potatoes, boiled and peeled
1 small onion, finely chopped
1–2 green chilies, finely chopped
½ tsp salt
½ tsp chili powder
5–6 tbsp tamarind juice (see page 16)
1 tbsp cilantro leaves, chopped

1 Cut the potatoes into 5 mm (¼ in) slices and
 cool thoroughly.
2 Gently mix in all the other ingredients. Serve cold.

Cheese Cutlet
(Paneer Cutlet)

Serves 4

1 tbsp ghee (see page 16)
250 ml (8 fl oz) milk
175 g (6 oz) paneer (see page 15), drained
100 g (4 oz) semolina
1 medium onion, finely chopped
2 green chilies, finely chopped
1 tbsp cilantro leaves, chopped
½ tsp salt
2 tbsp flour
120 ml (4 fl oz) milk
breadcrumbs
oil for deep frying

1 Heat the ghee in a karai over medium heat, add the milk, paneer, semolina, onion, chili, cilantro leaves and salt and mix thoroughly. Stirring constantly, cook until the mixture leaves the sides and a ball forms, about 3–4 minutes.

2 Spread the mixture 2 cm (¾ in) thick on a greased baking sheet. Cut into 2.5 cm (1 in) squares and chill for about 2 hours.

3 Make a smooth batter with the flour and milk. Dip each square in the batter and then roll it in breadcrumbs.

4 Heat the oil in a karai over high heat and fry the cutlets for 2–3 minutes until crisp and golden. Serve with chutney.

Deep-fried Pastry
(Nimki)

Serves 2

100 g (4 oz) flour
½ tsp salt
pinch of nigella seeds
pinch of ground roast cumin (see page 18)
1½ tbsp oil
about 50 ml (2 fl oz) hot water
oil for deep frying

1 Sift the flour and salt together. Mix in the nigella seeds and cumin. Rub in the oil.

2 Add enough water to make a stiff dough. Knead for 10 minutes until soft and smooth.

3 Divide the dough into 12 balls. Roll each ball into thin rounds 10 cm (4 in) across. Make 5 or 6 small cuts in the rounds.

4 Heat the oil in a karai over medium heat. Add a nimki and fry until crisp and golden. Drain on paper towels. Serve with chutney or Dry Potatoes (see page 61).

Lentil Cakes
(Dhokla)

Serves 4
225 g (8 oz) channa dal
4 tbsp water
3 green chilies
1 cm (½ in) ginger
1 tsp salt
pinch of turmeric
¾ tsp baking soda
juice of 1 lime
1 tbsp oil
½ tsp mustard seeds
pinch of asafetida
1 tbsp coconut, grated
1 tbsp cilantro leaves, chopped

1 Soak the channa dal overnight in plenty of cold water. The next morning, wash the dal two or three times.
2 Place the dal and the water in a food processor or blender and blend until smooth.
3 Grind the chilies and ginger together into a paste.
4 Add the chili and ginger paste, salt, turmeric, baking soda and lime juice to the blended dal and mix thoroughly.
5 Pour the mixture into a greased thali or a shallow cake tin, making sure that it does not come more than three-quarters of the way up.
6 Place the thali in a steamer, cover and steam for 20 minutes. Remove from the heat and set aside for 5 minutes. Insert a toothpick into the middle to test whether the dhoklas are cooked.
7 Cut into 4 cm (1½ in) squares and arrange on a plate.
8 Heat the oil in a small saucepan and add the mustard seeds; when they start to splutter, add the asafetida and, after 2–3 seconds, pour this over the dhoklas.
9 Garnish with the coconut and cilantro leaves.

Rolled Gram Flour Paste
(Khandvi)

Serves 4
175 g (6 oz) gram (chickpea) flour
4 tbsp yogurt
350 ml (12 fl oz) water
2 green chilies
1 cm (½ in) ginger
pinch of ground turmeric
¾ tsp salt
1 tbsp oil
½ tsp mustard seeds
pinch of asafetida
2 tbsp coconut, grated
2 tbsp cilantro leaves, chopped

1 Sift the gram flour into a large bowl.
2 Lightly beat the yogurt and water together.
3 Grind the chilies and ginger together to make a paste.
4 Add the yogurt and water mixture and the paste to the gram flour and whisk until smooth. Stir in the turmeric and salt. Put the mixture aside for 1 hour.
5 Pour the mixture into a saucepan and heat gently, stirring constantly until it thickens. (Be careful not to let any lumps form).
6 When the mixture thickens, spread a little thinly on a greased plate and let it cool. Try to roll it; if you cannot, thicken the mixture a little more.
7 Grease two or three large plates and spread the mixture very thinly on them with the back of a spatula. Allow the mixture to cool.
8 Cut into strips 5 mm (¼ in) long, and, starting at one end of each strip, roll them up. Place these rolls in a flat serving dish, next to each other.
9 Heat the oil until very hot. Add the mustard seeds and asafetida and let them sizzle for 8–10 seconds. Pour this over the rolled khandvi and garnish with the coconut and cilantro leaves.

Fried Lentil Patties
(Dal Vada)

Serves 4

225 g (8 oz) split black lentils, washed

5–6 curry leaves

2–3 green chilies

pinch of asafetida

1 cm (½ in) ginger, grated

¾ tsp cumin seeds

½ tsp salt

oil for deep frying

1 Soak the lentils in plenty of cold water overnight. Drain.

2 In a blender or food processor, blend the dal with all the other ingredients. Add a little water, if necessary, to make a fine, thick paste.

3 Heat the oil over medium high heat. Drop in a teaspoonful of the mixture and fry until nicely golden. Serve with a chutney as a snack or as an accompaniment to a main meal.

Samosas

Serves 4

Filling
3 tbsp oil
¼ tsp whole cumin seeds
450 g (1 lb) potatoes, diced into
   1 cm (½ in) cubes
1 green chili, finely chopped
pinch of turmeric
½ tsp salt
75 g (3 oz) peas
1 tsp ground roast cumin (see page 18)

Dough
225 g (8 oz) all-purpose flour
1 tsp salt
3 tbsp oil
about 100 ml (3 fl oz) hot water
oil for deep frying

1 To make the filling, heat the oil in a large saucepan over medium high heat and add the cumin seeds. Let them sizzle for a few seconds.
2 Add the potatoes and green chili and fry for 2–3 minutes. Add the turmeric and salt and, stirring occasionally, cook for 5 minutes.
3 Stir in the peas and the ground roast cumin. Cover, lower the heat and cook for 10 more minutes until the potatoes are tender. Cool.
4 To make the dough, sift together the flour and salt. Rub in the oil. Add enough water to form a stiff dough. Knead for 10 minutes until smooth.
5 Follow steps 1-7 on the opposite page to prepare and fill the samosas.
6 Heat the oil in a karai over medium heat. Put as many samosas as you can into the hot oil and fry until crisp and golden. Drain. Serve with a chutney.

Preparing the dough and filling the cones

1

Divide the dough into 12 balls.

2

Roll each ball into a round of about 15 cm (6 in) across.

3

Cut round in half.

4

Pick up one half, flatten it slightly and form a cone, sealing the overlapping edge with a little water.

5

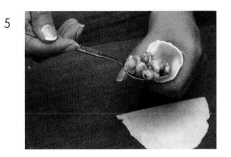

Fill the cone with 1½ tsp of the filling.

6

Seal the top of the cone with a little water.

7

Make all the samosas in the same way.

Yogurt Curry With Pakoras
(Karhi)

Serves 2
Pakoras

75 g (3 oz) gram flour	1 tbsp gram flour
¼ tsp salt	1 tbsp oil
pinch of ground turmeric	¼ tsp fenugreek seeds
	pinch of asafetida
about 4 tbsp water	6–8 curry leaves
oil for deep frying	2 green chilies, chopped

Curry

300 ml (½ pt) yogurt	½ tsp ground turmeric
350 ml (12 fl oz) water	½ tsp chili powder
	½ tsp salt

1 To make the pakoras, make a thick batter with the gram flour, salt, turmeric and water.
2 Heat the oil over medium high heat, drop in a teaspoonful of the batter and fry until crisp and golden. Drain and set aside.
3 To make the curry, whisk the yogurt, water and gram flour until smooth.
4 Place the fried pakoras in a bowl of water for 3–4 minutes. Gently squeeze out as much water as possible and put aside.
5 Heat 1 tbsp oil in a large saucepan over a medium heat. Add the fenugreek, asafetida, curry leaves and green chilies and let them sizzle for about 10 seconds.
6 Add the yogurt mixture, turmeric, chili powder and salt and slowly bring to a boil.
7 Lower the heat, add the pakoras and simmer for about 10 minutes until the sauce has thickened. Serve hot with rice.

Cucumber Salad
(Khamang Kakadi)

Serves 4
2 tbsp unsalted peanuts
½ cucumber, peeled and cut into fine strips
2 tbsp grated coconut
2 tbsp lemon juice
½ tsp salt
1 tbsp ghee (see page 16)
¼ tsp cumin seeds
pinch of asafetida
2 green chilies, chopped
1 tbsp cilantro leaves, chopped

1 Dry roast the peanuts and grind them into a fine powder.
2 Gently squeeze the cucumber to get rid of the excess water.
3 Place the cucumber, coconut, ground peanuts, lemon juice and salt in a bowl and mix gently.
4 In a small saucepan, heat the ghee. Add the cumin seeds and let them sizzle for 3–4 seconds. Add the asafetida and the green chilies and fry for 5–6 seconds. Pour this over the cucumber mixture and mix well.
5 Garnish with the cilantro leaves.

Cabbage Salad
(Kacha Pakka Kobi)

Serves 4
450 g (1 lb) green cabbage
1 tsp oil
2 green chilies, chopped
2 tsp split black lentils
½ tsp mustard seeds
pinch of asafetida
¾ tsp coconut, grated
1 tbsp cilantro leaves, chopped

1 Cut the cabbage very finely into long strips. Wash and dry them.
2 Heat the oil in a large saucepan over medium high heat. Add the chilies and fry for 3–4 seconds.
3 Remove the saucepan from the heat, add the lentils and stirfry until lightly golden (this will only take a few seconds).
4 Put the saucepan back on the heat and add the mustard seeds; after 8–10 seconds add the asafetida and fry for 2–3 seconds.
5 Add the cabbage and salt and, stirring constantly, cook for 3–4 minutes. Serve garnished with the coconut and cilantro leaves.

Spicy Sago
(Saboodana Ki Khichiri)

Serves 4

175 g (6 oz) sago

75 g (3 oz) peanuts, skinned

2 tbsp oil

1 tsp mustard seeds

2 green chilies, chopped

pinch of asafetida

good pinch of turmeric

1 tsp salt

1 tsp sugar

about 5 tbsp water

juice of ½ a lime

1 tbsp coconut, grated

1 tbsp cilantro leaves, chopped

1 Wash the sago and soak in a little water for about 10 minutes. Drain and dry on paper towels.

2 Roast the peanuts and grind coarsely.

3 Mix the sago and peanuts.

4 Heat the oil in a saucepan over medium high heat. Add the mustard seeds and green chilies; when the mustard seeds start to splutter, add the asafetida and fry for 2–3 seconds.

5 Add the sago and peanut mixture, turmeric, salt and sugar and stirfry for 1 minute.

6 Lower the heat and continue to stirfry for another 2–3 minutes.

7 Add the water, cover and cook, stirring occasionally, until the sago is tender and nearly dry.

8 Add the lime juice and give it a good stir. Serve garnished with the coconut and cilantro leaves.

Melon with Orange Juice
(Tarbuch Aur Mosamki Ka Rus)

Serves 4
1 honeydew melon
15 g (½ oz) butter or ghee (see page 16)
½ tsp ground cumin
juice of 2 sweet oranges
1 tbsp lemon juice
2 tbsp sugar

1 Cut the melon into segments, remove the pulp, seeds and skin. Cut into cubes.
2 Heat the butter or ghee in a pan, add the cumin and let it sizzle until the fragrance emerges.
3 Meanwhile, mix the orange and lemon juice with the sugar and 1 tbsp water.
4 Sprinkle the syrup on the melon, add the cumin and serve.

Tomato Salad
(Kachumbar)

Serves 4
450 g (1 lb) tomatoes, sliced
2 green chilies, finely sliced
2 tsp sugar
1 tbsp lemon juice
leaves from 1 or 2 sprigs of cilantro
salt

1 Mix the tomato with the chili.
2 Sprinkle with sugar, lemon juice and cilantro leaves. Mix well and add salt to taste.

Chicken and Vegetable Salad
(Murghi Aur Kachumbar)

Serves 4–6

225 g (8 oz) cooked chicken, cut into
    bite-sized pieces
1 or 2 apples, cored and cut into segments
75 g (3 oz) white cabbage, grated
2 tomatoes, cut into 8 pieces
1 green chili, finely chopped
½ tsp ground black pepper
¼ tsp ground nutmeg
salt
2 tbsp lemon juice
1 or 2 sprigs of cilantro

1 Mix the chicken with the apple, cabbage, tomato and green chili.
2 Sprinkle on the pepper, nutmeg and salt.
3 Squeeze over the lemon juice and toss the salad. Garnish with cilantro leaves.

Cabbage Fritters
(Gobi Pakoras)

Serves 4

100 g (4 oz) gram flour
100 g (4 oz) hard white cabbage, grated
1 small onion, finely sliced
2 green chilies, thinly sliced
5 g (½ oz) fresh ginger, finely grated
4–6 curry leaves, chopped
1 tsp salt
½ tsp chili powder
½ tsp garam masala (see page 17)
oil for deep frying

1 Mix the flour with 150 ml (5 fl oz pt) water to make a batter.
2 Add all the ingredients except the oil and stir well to coat.
3 Heat oil for deep frying, add the cabbage in batter by the tablespoonful and fry until golden. Drain on absorbent paper towels.
4 Serve with chutney.

CHUTNEYS AND PICKLES

Pickles and chutneys can be spicy, sweet, tart, hot, sour, mild or aromatic. The more variety, the better. They are best served with plain foods such as rice and bread, or with lightly spiced dishes. They should not have to compete with the flavor of the dish they accompany, and they should certainly not overwhelm it. A yogurt chutney called raita is often served to provide a cooling contrast to a hot spicy meal.

Yogurt with Cucumber
(Kheera Raita)

325 ml (11 fl oz) natural yogurt
1–2 green chilies, chopped
2 tbsp chopped cilantro leaves
½ cucumber, finely sliced
½ tsp chili powder
½ tsp ground roast cumin (see page 18)
½ tsp salt

1 Place the yogurt in a bowl and whisk until smooth.
2 Add all the other ingredients and stir well. Chill.

Yogurt with Mini Dumplings
(Boondi Raita)

75 g (3 oz) boondi (gram flour balls)
325 ml (11 fl oz) natural yogurt
½ tsp salt
½ tsp chili powder
pinch of paprika
pinch of garam masala (see page 7)

1 Soak the boondi in a little cold water for 10–15 minutes.
2 Beat the yogurt in a bowl until smooth. Add the salt and chili powder and stir.
3 Gently squeeze the boondi to remove the water and add to the spiced yogurt. Mix well and chill. Before serving sprinkle with paprika and garam masala.

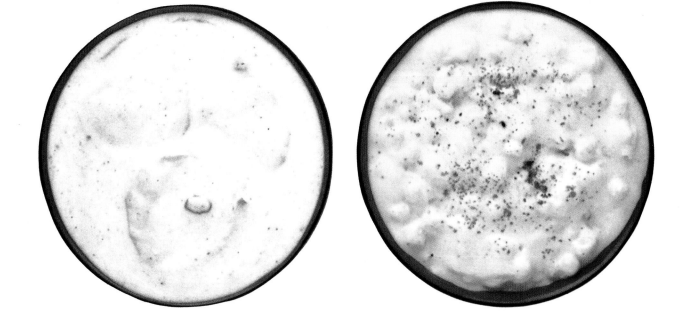

Yogurt with Potatoes
(Aloo Raita)

450 ml (15 fl oz) natural yogurt
275 g (10 oz) potatoes, boiled and diced into
    5 mm (¼ in) cubes
1 small onion, finely chopped
½ tsp salt
¼ tsp ground black pepper
½ tsp ground roast cumin (see page 18)
1 green chili, chopped
1 tbsp cilantro leaves

1   Beat the yogurt in a bowl until smooth.
2   Add the potatoes, onion, salt, pepper and cumin
    and gently mix. Chill.
3   Serve sprinkled with the chili and
    cilantro leaves.

Yogurt with Eggplant
(Baigan Raita)

6–8 tbsp oil
1 small eggplant, cut into small pieces
325 ml (12 fl oz) natural yogurt
½ tsp salt
½ tsp ground roast cumin (see page 18)
½ tsp chili powder

1   Heat the oil in a karai and fry the eggplant pieces
    until brown. Drain.
2   Place the yogurt in a bowl and whisk until smooth.
    Add the salt, cumin and chili and mix thoroughly.
3   Place the fried eggplant in a bowl and pour over
    the spiced yogurt. Chill.

Yogurt and Tomato Relish
(Tamatar Raita)

100 g (4 oz) tomatoes, diced
½ cucumber, quartered lengthways and sliced
1 small onion, finely chopped
150 ml (¼ pt) natural yogurt
leaves from 1 sprig of cilantro
1 green chili, finely chopped
15 g (½ oz) fresh ginger, finely grated
½ tsp salt
1 tsp mustard seeds, roasted without fat

1 Mix the tomato and cucumber with the onion. You can reduce the strength of the onion by rinsing it in hot water, if preferred.
2 Mix the yogurt with the remaining ingredients. Stir the dressing into the vegetables and add extra salt to taste.

Coconut Chutney
(Thankai Chutney)

100 g (4 oz) finely grated coconut
3 red chilies, chopped and seeded
50 ml (2 fl oz) natural yogurt
1 tbsp oil
½ tsp mustard seeds
4 curry leaves
salt

1 Grind, pound or blend the coconut and 2 red chilies in a blender, then stir in the yogurt.
2 Heat the oil, add the mustard seeds and fry until they have all popped, then add the remaining red chili and the curry leaves and continue to fry for 2–3 minutes.
3 Add to the coconut mix with salt to taste.

Tamarind Chutney
(Imli Chutney)

1 tbsp cilantro seeds
1 tsp black peppercorns
½ tsp cumin seeds
½ tsp fenugreek seeds
1 tsp mustard seeds
½ tsp asafetida
5 red chilies
2–3 tbsp oil
1 tsp polished split black lentils (urid dal)
1 tsp channa dal soaked for 20 minutes,
    then drained
6 curry leaves
25 g (1 oz) shelled peanuts
juice from 225 g (8 oz) seedless tamarind
    (see page 16)
2 tbsp brown sugar
salt
1 tbsp sesame seeds
25–50 g (1–2 oz) dried coconut

1   Heat a frying pan without any butter or oil and add the cilantro, peppercorns, cumin, fenugreek, half of the mustard seeds, half of the asafetida and 4 red chilies. Roast the spices for about 5 minutes, shaking the pan to prevent burning. Pound or grind the spices into a fine powder and set aside.
2   Heat the oil in a pan, add the remaining mustard seeds, urid and channa dals, curry leaves and remaining chili, cut into 3 or 4 pieces, and fry until all the seeds have popped.
3   Add the peanuts and fry for another 3 or 4 minutes, then add the tamarind juice, the roast spice powder, sugar, ½ tsp salt and the remaining asafetida.
4   Heat another saucepan without fat or oil, roast the sesame seeds and coconut and add to the chutney. Stir well, adding extra salt to taste.

Tomato, Onion and Cucumber Chutney
(Kachumbar)

1 large cucumber, finely chopped
4 medium onions, finely chopped
2 large tomatoes, finely chopped
2 green chilies, finely chopped
5–6 chopped cilantro leaves
2–3 tbsp lime juice
1 tsp salt

1   Mix all the ingredients together.
2   Chill for 2–3 hours before serving.

Sweet Tomato Chutney
(Tamatar Ki Chutney)

450 g (1 lb) tomatoes
50 g (2 oz) sugar
½ tsp ground cardamom seeds
3 cloves
½ tsp chili powder
1 tbsp oil
½ tsp mustard seeds
1 tbsp white wine vinegar
salt
4 curry leaves

1 Immerse the tomatoes in a bowl of boiling water for about 2 minutes, until the skins split, then drain them, leave to cool, peel and chop.
2 Bring 150 ml (5 fl oz) of water to a boil in a small pan, add the sugar and tomato and cook for 5 minutes, stirring.
3 Add the cardamom, cloves and chili powder and continue cooking, mashing the tomato under the back of a wooden spoon to make a thick paste. Remove the saucepan from the heat.
4 Heat the oil, add the mustard seeds and fry until they have all popped, then add to the tomato.
5 Stir in the vinegar, add salt to taste and sprinkle the curry leaves on top.

Peanut Soy Sauce
(Seng Dana Chutney)

100 g (4 oz) shelled peanuts, skinned
2 red chilies, cut into 3 or 4 pieces
½ tsp salt
2 tbsp soy sauce
1 tbsp lemon juice
1 tbsp brown sugar
2 tbsp oil

1 Pound, grind or blend the first six ingredients in a blender.
2 Heat the oil in a pan, add the peanut mix, cook until it begins to bubble, then take off the heat and stir well.

Green Cilantro Chutney
(Hari Dhaniya Chutney)

leaves from 3–4 sprigs cilantro
1 or 2 green chilies
15 g (½ oz) fresh ginger, grated
salt
2 tbsp lemon juice
½ tsp sugar

1 Grind, pound or blend the cilantro leaves, green chili, ginger and ½ tsp salt in a blender to make a thick paste.
2 Stir in the lemon juice and add sugar and extra salt to taste.

Mint Chutney
(Poodina Ki Chutney)

handful mint leaves, washed
50 ml (2 fl oz) tamarind juice
2 tbsp chopped onions
2 cloves garlic
2 cm (¾ in) ginger
2–3 green chilies
½ tsp salt
½ tsp sugar

1 Blend all the ingredients together until you have a smooth paste.

Chutney can be stored in an airtight container in the fridge for up to one week.

Green Mango Relish
(Aam Chutney)

225 g (8 oz) hard green mango
50 g (2 oz) finely grated coconut
red chili or 1 tsp chili powder
1 tsp mustard seeds
1 tbsp yogurt
1 tbsp oil
4 curry leaves
salt

1 Chop the mango as finely as possible, with or without the skin.
2 Grind, pound or blend the coconut, chili and half the mustard seeds in a blender, add to the mango and stir in the yogurt.
3 Heat the oil in a pan, add the remaining mustard seeds and the curry leaves and fry until all the seeds have popped, then stir into the relish. Add salt to taste.

Black Lentil Curry
(Urid Dal Chutney)

75–100 g (3–4 oz) polished split black lentils (urid dal)
1 or 2 red chilies
1 tsp asafetida
50 g (2 oz) finely grated coconut
juice from 25 g (1 oz) seedless tamarind (see page 16)
salt

1 Pick over the dal. Heat a saucepan without fat or oil, add the dal, 1 chili and the asafetida and cook, shaking the saucepan to prevent burning, until the dal is golden.
2 Pound the roast spices together.
3 Grind, pound or blend the coconut and tamarind in a blender with 1–2 tbsp water, then add the roast spice powder and grind them together, adding a little more water if necessary.
4 Add salt to taste.

DESSERTS

India offers a large variety of desserts and sweets. Indian desserts are often the climax of a meal and are much anticipated by diners. Most sweets are milk based and can be prepared in advance.

Ice Cream with Almonds and Pistachio Nuts
(Kulfi)

Serves 6
1.2 l (2½ pt) milk
50 g (2 oz) sugar
2 tbsp ground almonds
2 tbsp pistachio nuts, skinned and chopped
few drops rosewater

1 Bring the milk to a boil, stirring constantly.
2 Lower the heat and simmer, stirring occasionally, until it reduces to about 500 ml (17 fl oz).
3 Add the sugar and mix thoroughly. Continue to simmer for another 2–3 minutes. Remove from the heat and let it cool completely.
4 Add the almonds and mix into the thickened milk, making sure no lumps form.
5 Stir in the pistachios and rosewater.
6 Place the mixture in a dish, cover it with a lid or foil and place it in the freezer.
7 Take it out of the freezer after 20 minutes and give it a good stir to break up the ice crystals. Repeat twice more.
8 After this, it may be divided up into six chilled single dishes, and covered and frozen for about 4–5 hours. Take it out of the freezer about 10 minutes before you are ready to serve. An alternative serving suggestion would be to prepare the ice cream as individual popsicles, as seen below.

Pumpkin Halva
(Pethi Halva)

Serves 4
450 g (1 lb) pumpkin
600 ml (1 pt) milk
150 g (5 oz) sugar
1 tsp rosewater
100 g (4 oz) ghee (see page 16)
¼ tsp ground cardamom seeds
10–15 cashew nuts, halved

1 Scrape the seeds and pulp from the inside of the pumpkin, cut the flesh from the skin and chop into chunks.
2 Grate the pumpkin coarsely, put in a muslin cloth and squeeze out all the moisture.
3 Put the pumpkin in a saucepan with the milk, sugar and rosewater and cook over low heat for 30 minutes or more, stirring briskly, until all the milk has evaporated.
4 Stir in the ghee and continue cooking until it separates. Drain off any butter not absorbed by the pumpkin mixture.
5 Stir in the cardamom and cashews and spread the mixture in a greased dish with straight sides, in one layer about 5 cm (2 in) deep.
6 Leave for about 45 minutes, until set, then cut into squares.

Mango Soufflé
(Aam Pudding)

Serves 4
4 eggs
2 tsp gelatin
300 ml (10 fl oz) mango juice or 225 g (8 oz) mango pulp
2 tsp sugar
salt
2 tbsp superfine sugar
½ tsp vanilla extract

1 Separate the eggs, putting the yolks into a mixing bowl.
2 In a small bowl, mix the gelatin with 3 tbsp water.
3 Beat the yolks well and mix thoroughly with the mango juice or pulp.
4 Stir in the granulated sugar, gelatin and ½ tsp salt.
5 Put the mixing bowl over a saucepan of boiling water, making sure that the bowl does not touch the water or the eggs will scramble. Beat the mixture for 10 minutes, then remove from the heat.
6 Whisk the egg whites with ½ tsp salt and the superfine sugar until stiff, then fold into the yolks, adding the vanilla extract.
7 Divide the mixture between four small dishes and chill before serving.

South Indian Creamed Rice
(Payasam)

Serves 4
90 g (4 oz) short grain white rice
1.2 l (2½ pt) milk
75 g (3 oz) jaggery (raw palm sugar) or
  brown sugar
1 tbsp cashew nuts, roasted

1 Wash the rice and set aside in a sieve to drain for 20 minutes.
2 Bring the milk to a boil in a large saucepan, stirring constantly.
3 Lower the heat, add the rice and stir well to mix.
4 Simmer until the rice is tender and the milk slightly thickened.
5 Add the jaggery or brown sugar, stir to mix and simmer for a further 5–7 minutes.
6 Stir in the cashews and remove from the heat.

Beetroot Halva
(Chukander Halva)

Serves 4
450 g (1 lb) beets
600 ml (1 pt) milk
175 g (6 oz) sugar
100 g (4 oz) ghee (see page 16)
¼ tsp ground cardamom seeds
10 almonds

1 Scrape the skin from the beets, then grate coarsely.
2 Put the beets in a saucepan with the milk and sugar and cook gently for 30 minutes or more, stirring briskly, until all the milk has evaporated.
3 Add the ghee, cardamom and almonds and continue cooking, stirring all the time, until the mixture is heavy and sticky.
4 Spread the mixture in a greased dish with straight sides, in one layer about 5 cm (2 in) deep.
5 Leave for about 45 minutes to set, then cut into squares.

Steamed Plantain Cake
(Kela Gâteau)

Serves 4
175–225 g (6–8 oz) self-rising flour
1 tbsp ghee (see page 16)
50 g (2 oz) finely grated coconut
175 g (6 oz) brown sugar
½ tsp ground cardamom seeds
3 or 4 ripe plantains, peeled and thinly sliced

1 Sift the flour into a bowl, make a well in the middle and pour in the ghee. Gradually adding as little warm water as possible (about 6 tbsp), work the ingredients into a smooth dough.
2 Mix the plantain with the remaining ingredients.
3 Cut foil into 4 x 23 cm (9 in) squares and divide the dough between them. With your finger or a spoon, dipped in water to prevent sticking, spread the dough out to within 2.5 cm (1 in) of each side of the square.
4 Divide the plantain mixture between the sheets of dough and spread to cover.
5 Fold each foil sheet over in the middle and fold over the edges, pressing down well to seal.
6 Put the foil parcels in a steamer over a saucepan of boiling water and steam, covered, for 25–30 minutes, making sure that the foil does not touch the water.

Creamed Rice
(Kheer)

Serves 4
2 tbsp basmati rice
1.2 l (2½ pt) milk
65 g (2½ oz) sugar
2 tbsp peeled almonds
¼ tsp ground cardamom
1 tsp rosewater

1 Wash the rice in several changes of water and soak in plenty of water for 30 minutes. Drain.

2 Bring the milk to a boil over high heat, stirring constantly. Lower the heat and simmer for 30 minutes, stirring occasionally.

3 Add the drained rice and sugar and continue to cook for 30–40 minutes until the milk has thickened and the rice is very soft and disintegrated.

4 Add the almonds and continue to cook for 10 more minutes.

5 Remove from the heat and stir in the cardamom and rosewater.

6 Place in a serving dish and refrigerate. Serve chilled.

Plantain Jaggery
(Kela Gur)

Serves 4
4 ripe plantains, unpeeled
175 g (6 oz) jaggery (raw palm sugar) or brown sugar)

1 Cut the plantain into 5 cm (2 in) lengths, put in a saucepan and add just enough water to cover.

2 Add the jaggery and cook for 35–40 minutes, until all the water has evaporated.

3 Leave to cool, peel, then chill and serve cold.

Flatbread Stuffed with Sweetened Legumes
(Puran Poon)

Serves 4

Filling	Dough
225 g (8 oz) channa dal	225 g (8 oz) whole
about 750 ml	wheat flour
(1½ pt) water	1 tbsp oil
225 g (8 oz) sugar	about 120 ml (4 fl oz)
½ tsp ground	hot water
cardamom	ghee (see page 16)
½ tsp saffron	

1 To make the filling, wash the channa dal in several changes of water.
2 In a large saucepan, bring the dal and water to a boil over medium high heat. Lower the heat, cover, leaving the lid slightly open, and simmer for about 1¼ hours until soft and thick. Remove from the heat.
3 Add the sugar, cardamom and saffron and stir well to mix thoroughly.
4 Return the saucepan to the heat and, stirring constantly, cook until thick and dry. Cool.
5 To make the dough, sift the flour and rub in the oil.
6 Add enough water to make a stiff dough. Knead for about 8–10 minutes until soft and smooth.
7 Divide the dough into 10–12 balls.
8 Take a ball, flatten it on a lightly floured surface and roll into a round of 7.5 cm (3 in) across. Place 1 tbsp of the filling in the center and fold up the edges, enclosing the filling completely. Gently roll into a round 18 cm (7 in) across.
9 Place in a hot frying pan and cook over on medium heat for 1–2 minutes on each side until brown spots appear.
10 Brush with ghee and serve hot.

Cheese Fudge
(Sandesh)

Serves 4

350 g (12 oz) paneer (see page 15), drained
75 g (3 oz) sugar
1 tbsp pistachio nuts, finely chopped

1 Place the paneer on a plate and rub with the palm of your hand until smooth and creamy.
2 Put the paneer in a karai over medium heat, add the sugar and, stirring constantly, cook until it leaves the sides and forms a ball.
3 Remove from the heat and spread on a plate 1 cm (1 in) thick. Cool slightly, sprinkle with the nuts and cut into small diamonds. Serve warm or hot.

Semolina Halva
(Sooji Halva)

Serves 4

3 tbsp ghee (see page 16)
25 g (1 oz) almonds, blanched and sliced
100 g (4 oz) semolina
1 tbsp raisins
400 ml (14 fl oz) milk
65 g (2½ oz) sugar

1 Heat the ghee in a karai over medium heat.
2 Add the almonds and fry for 1–2 minutes until golden brown. Remove with a slotted spoon and drain on paper towel.
3 Put in the semolina and fry, stirring continuously, until golden. Add the raisins and mix with the semolina.
4 Add the milk and sugar and continue stirring until the mixture leaves the sides of the karai and a ball forms.
5 Serve on a flat dish decorated with the almonds.

Gujarati-style Creamed Rice (Doodh Pak)

Serves 4

1.2 l (2½ pt) milk
25 g (1 oz) rice
40 g (1½ oz) sugar
½ tsp ground cardamom
1 tbsp ground almonds

1 Bring the milk to a boil, stirring constantly.
2 Add the rice and sugar; stir to mix. Lower the heat, and, stirring occasionally, simmer until the milk has thickened and is reduced to about 500 ml (17 fl oz).
3 Remove from the heat and stir in the cardamom and almonds, making sure no lumps form when the nuts are added. Serve with hot Poori (see page 112).

Baked Yogurt (Payodhi)

Serves 4

410 g (14¼ oz) can evaporated milk
397 g (14 oz) can condensed milk
500 ml (17 fl oz) yogurt
1 tbsp pistachio nuts, skinned and chopped
handful of almonds, to decorate

1 Preheat the oven to 225°C/450°F/Gas Mark 5.
2 Whisk the evaporated milk, condensed milk and yogurt together for 1 minute.
3 Pour into an ovenproof dish and place in the preheated oven.
4 Turn the oven off after 6 minutes and leave the dish in the oven overnight.
5 Chill. Serve decorated with the chopped pistachios and almonds (see picture below).

Gram Flour Balls
(Besan Laddu)

Serves 4

175 g (6 oz) gram (chickpea) flour
6 tbsp ghee (see page 16)
100 g (4 oz) sugar
1 tbsp chopped pistachios

1 Sift the gram flour.
2 Heat the ghee in a heavy-based saucepan over medium heat and fry the gram flour until golden.
3 Remove from the heat and cool. Add sugar and mix well.
4 When cold, make into small balls about the size of a walnut. Roll each ball in the chopped pistachios.

Yogurt with Saffron
(Shrikhand)

Serves 4
600 ml (1 pt) yogurt
¼ tsp saffron
1 tbsp warm milk
100 g (4 oz) superfine sugar
2 tbsp pistachio nuts, skinned and chopped

1 Put the yogurt in a muslin bag and hang it up for 4–5 hours to get rid of the excess water.
2 Soak the saffron in the milk for 30 minutes.
3 Whisk the drained yogurt, sugar and saffron milk together until smooth and creamy.
4 Put in a dish and garnish with the nuts. Chill until set.

Fritters in Syrup
(Malpoa)

Serves 4
200 g (7 oz) all-purpose flour
1½ tsp baking powder
175 ml (6 fl oz) yogurt
about 175 ml (6 fl oz) milk
225 g (8 oz) sugar
450 ml (15 fl oz) water
oil for deep frying

1 Sift the flour and baking powder together. Mix in the yogurt. Add enough milk to make a thick batter.
2 Boil the sugar and water together for 10 minutes.
3 Heat the oil in a karai over medium high heat. Drop in 1 tbsp of the batter at a time and fry until crisp and brown. Drain on paper towels.
4 Soak the fried malpoa in the syrup for 5 minutes. Serve in a little syrup, hot or cold.

Saffron Rice
(Zaffrani Chawal)

Serves 4–6
275 g (10 oz) basmati rice
½ tsp saffron
about 1 l (2 pt) boiling water
5 tbsp ghee (see page 16)
2–3 cardamom pods
50 g (2 oz) almonds, slivered
65 g (2½ oz) sugar
1 tbsp pistachio nuts, chopped

1 Wash the rice and soak in water for 15 minutes. Drain thoroughly. Soak the saffron in 2 tbsp of the boiling water for 15 minutes.
2 Heat the ghee in a large saucepan over medium high heat; add the cardamom pods and sizzle for 3–4 seconds. Add the rice and almonds and, stirring constantly, fry until lightly golden.
3 Add the boiling water, saffron and sugar and stir. Turn the heat down low, cover and cook for about 20 minutes until all the water has been absorbed and the rice is tender. Fluff with a fork, garnish with pistachios and serve.

Cheese Balls in Syrup
(Rassogolla)

Serves 4
300 g (11 oz) paneer (see page 15), drained
175 g (6 oz) ricotta cheese
350 g (12 oz) sugar
1.25 l (2½ pt) water

1 Rub the paneer and ricotta cheese with the palms of your hands until smooth and creamy. Divide into 16 balls.
2 Boil the sugar and water for 5 minutes over medium heat. Put the balls in the syrup and boil for 40 minutes.
3 Cover and continue to boil for another 30 minutes. Serve warm or cold.

Rice Pudding
(Choler Payesh)

Serves 4
1.2 l (2½ pt) milk
1 tbsp basmati rice, washed
2 tbsp sugar
2 tbsp raisins
1 tsp ground cardamom

1　Bring the milk to a boil in a large pan, stirring continuously.

2　Lower the heat and simmer for 20 minutes. Add the rice and sugar and continue simmering for another 35–40 minutes until the milk has thickened and reduced to 600 ml (1 pt). While cooking, stir occasionally to stop the milk sticking to the bottom of the pan.

3　Add 1 tbsp raisins and ½ tsp ground cardamom and, stirring constantly, cook for 3–4 more minutes.

4　Remove from the heat and garnish with the remaining raisins and ground cardamom. Serve hot or cold.

Khir with Oranges
(Kamla Khir)

Serves 4
1.2 l (2½ pt) milk
40 g (1½ oz) sugar
2 oranges, peeled

1   Boil the milk in a large saucepan, stirring constantly. Add the sugar and stir. Reduce heat and, stirring occasionally, simmer until has reduced to 450 ml (15 fl oz). Cool.
2   Remove all the pith from the oranges and slice. Add to the cooled milk. Serve chilled.

Fried Sweets in Syrup
(Jalebi)

Serves 4
150 g (5 oz) all-purpose flour
½ tsp baking powder
a little milk
2 tbsp water
275 g (10 oz) sugar
250 ml (8 fl oz) water
few drops yellow food coloring
few drops rosewater
oil for deep frying

1   Sift the flour and baking powder together. Add enough milk to make a thick batter of pouring consistency. Set aside in a warm place overnight.
2   When you are ready to fry the jalebis, prepare the syrup. Place the sugar and water in a large saucepan and bring to a boil. Boil for 5–6 minutes until it becomes slightly thick. Remove from the heat and add coloring and rosewater. Stir well and set aside.
3   Heat the oil over medium high heat.
4   Place the batter in a piping bag with a 5 mm (¼ in) plain nozzle. Squeeze the batter into the hot oil, making spiral shapes of about 6 cm (2½ in) in diameter.
5   Fry until golden. Drain and add to the syrup for 1 minute. Remove from the syrup.

Carrot Halva
(Gajar Halva)

Serves 4

450 g (1 lb) carrots, peeled and grated
900 ml (2 pt) milk
150 g (5 oz) sugar
3 green cardamom pods
4 tbsp ghee (see page 16)
2 tbsp raisins
2 tbsp pistachio nuts, skinned and chopped

1   Place the carrots, milk, sugar and cardamom pods in a large saucepan and bring to a boil. Lower the heat to medium low and, stirring occasionally, cook until all the liquid has evaporated.

2   Heat the ghee in a large frying pan over medium heat, add the cooked carrots, raisins and pistachios and, stirring constantly, fry for 15–20 minutes until the mixture is dry and reddish in color. Serve hot or cold.

GLOSSARY

Adrak Fresh ginger (see below).

Amchur Dried mango powder. Has a bittersweet flavor.

Asafetida A truffle-flavored brown resin, available in powdered or lump form, and is often used in cooking with beans. If you buy the lump form, crumble off a small piece and crush it between two sheets of paper.

Basmati rice The finest Indian long-grained rice, grown in the foothills of the Himalayas.

Besan Also known as gram flour, this is the flour made from chickpeas. It is used particularly in the south for making pancakes and steamed patties.

Biriyani A rice and vegetable, meat or seafood oven-cooked dish.

Boondi Small deep-fried balls made out of gram flour.

Cardamom Both black and green cardamoms are available, although the black ones are not often available. They are large and hairy. Use the green ones for the recipes in this book.

Channa dal A very versatile dried split pea. It looks like an ordinary yellow split pea, but is smaller with a sweeter, nuttier flavor. It can be cooked until soft for the dish called simply "dal," or, as in southern India, it can be used as a spice.

Chawal Rice.

Chickpeas Also called gram or garbanzo beans. Because chickpeas often demand hours of cooking before they become tender, it is often cheaper to buy them canned.

Chilies Can be bought fresh, in which case they are normally green, or dried, in which case they are red. Chilies are very hot and should be handled with care and used according to taste.

Cinnamon Can be bought powdered, or, better, in sticks. These sticks are the rolled bark of the cinnamon tree and have a warm spicy flavor.

Coconut Characteristic of the cooking of southern India. Buy a fresh coconut to extract the milk (see page 18) or use dried coconut to thicken sauces or garnish finished dishes. Dried coconut can be bought in most supermarkets and delicatessens.

Cilantro Both the seeds and leaves of this plant are used. Also known as cilantro, it can be grown as easily as parsley. The seeds are small and round and are used either whole or ground. The leaves are bright green and have a strong bittersweet flavor.

Cumin seeds White or black, these seeds can be used whole or ground.

Curry leaves Can sometimes be bought fresh, which is preferable to using them dried. Used extensively in the south of India, they are mainly added to food just before it is ready.

Dahi Yogurt.

Dalchini Cinnamon (see above).

Dals Dried split peas, usually bought skinned.

Dhaniya Cilantro (see above).

Elaichi Cardamom (see above).

Fenugreek seeds Chunky, tawny-colored seeds, often used roasted and ground. They have a bitter taste. Fenugreek leaves are a vegetable used like spinach, to which the plant is related.

Garam masala A mixture of spices ground together (see page 17), it is sprinkled on some dishes after they have been cooked.

Ghee Drawn butter. It can be made at home (see page 16) and does not need to be refrigerated.

Ginger Fresh ginger (adrak) is a fawn-colored rhizome. Ginger can also be bought powdered (soondth).

Gosht Meat. Goat is the meat most often eaten in India.

Gram flour Made from chickpeas and also known as besan.

Haldi Turmeric (see below).

Halva A sweet dish.

Hing Asafetida (see above).

Imli Tamarind (see below).

Jaggery Raw sugar, eaten as it is and used to flavor various dishes, even vegetable curries.

Jeera Cumin (see above).

Jingha Shrimp.

Kofta Meat or banana balls.

Kumban Mushroom.

Lassi A yogurt drink (see page 16).

Luong Cloves.

Machi Fish.

Masala Spices.

Masoor dal Skinned split red lentils.

Moong dal Skinned split mung beans.

Murghi Chicken.

Mustard oil A yellow oil made from mustard seeds that is pungent when raw and sweet when heated. Often used in Kashmir and Bengal.

Mustard seeds Small yellow or black seeds often popped in hot oil, when they have a nutty sweet flavor. When ground for mustard powder their character is quite different – hot and smarting.

Nigella seeds Tiny triangular-shaped black seeds known as kalonji in India and used in cooking. They are commonly seen studded on some Indian breads.

Narial Coconut (see above).

Neem Curry leaves (see above).

Panch phoron Also known as Bengali five-spice, this is a mixture of five spices. The five spices are: fenugreek, nigella seeds, cumin seeds, black mustard seeds and fennel seeds in equal parts.

Papaya A fruit with good digestive properties.

Pilaf Fried rice dish.

Raita A cooling side dish made with yogurt.

Roti Bread.

Sago Edible starch that is extracted from the sago palm. It is dried to produce a flour or processed into a granular form.

Sambar powder A southern Indian spice mix for vegetable curries (see page 11).

Soondth Powdered ginger (see above).

Tamarind The bean-like fruit of the tamarind tree, often used in southern Indian cooking.

Tava A flat cast-iron pan used for making bread.

Thali A large tray, often of wrought metal.

Toran A style of cooking where the dish remains dry.

Toovar dal A glossy dark yellow split pea.

Urid dal Polished split black lentils, often used as a spice in southern India.

Vark Silver and gold leaf used to decorate food on special occasions. It is edible.

Vindaloo A highly spiced and hot curry, traditionally from Goa.

Index

Acknowledgements

The publishers would like to thank the following picture libraries for their kind permission to use their pictures:

Istock: 18, 23, 38, 69, 76, 77, 119, 151,
Shutterstock: 8, 9, 10, 11, 16, 17, 21, 25, 29, 31, 35, 37, 41, 42, 46, 49, 51, 54, 56, 61, 62, 64, 66. 68, 71, 75, 78, 79, 80, 82, 85, 89, 90, 92, 98, 99, 100, 101, 103, 104, 105, 106, 114, 115, 118, 122, 134, 125, 131, 132, 135, 137, 139, 143, 145, 147, 150, 153, 154, 156, 158, 159, 163, 164, 167, 169
Photocuisine: 45, 96
Stock food: front cover

Every effort has been made to contact the copyright holders for images reproduced in this book. The Publisher would welcome any errors or omissions being brought to their attention and apologizes in advance for any unintentional omissions or errors. The Publisher will be pleased to insert the appropriate acknowledgment to any companies or individuals in any subsequent edition of the work.